CLINICAL GESTALT THERAPY

CLINICAL GESTALT THERAPY

Yevgeny Ryaboy

A Manual

Translated by Olena Khavkina

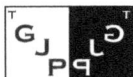

A Publication of the Gestalt Journal Press

Translation: Olena Khavkina

Cover design by Molly Rawle

CONTENTS

Preface. 7

Acknowledgments.. 11

Introduction to Clinical Gestalt Therapy.. 13

Notes on the Terms Used. 17

Notes on the Idea of Psychopathology in Gestalt. 21

Chapter 1. 27
  Gestalt Approach to Work with Nosogenies
In Children and Adolescents

Chapter 2. 43
  Projection and Delusion

Chapter 3. 55
  Gestalt Therapy in the World of Histrionic Suffering

Afterward. 83

About the Author. 85

Review by Yaro Starak.. 87

Bibliography. 89

PREFACE

In order to write a good book on clinical Gestalt Therapy, it is important for it to be Relevant. The author should be aware of the process of writing it and the final result. The author should also approach this matter with all their Responsibility.

While working on the text, I tried not to forget about these three fundamental values of Gestalt Therapy: Relevance, Awareness[1], and Responsibility. They guided me on my journey in the world of psychopathology.

To write a professional book is an existential challenge. The origins of this challenge can be found somewhere in the distant year of 2013. At that time, I had already successfully completed my certification in Gestalt Therapy, worked conscientiously and selflessly as a psychologist in a general psychiatric hospital for about 5 years and was developing a private psychotherapy practice.

At that period, I was also working at the university giving lectures on clinical psychology, in which I was completely immersed.

---

[1] **Awareness** is a mental state that involves observing one's sensory signals, feelings, and thoughts that arise in the moment and then accepting them. However, awareness is never identical to introspection, since it is both a certain experience and contemplation of what is happening with a person in contact with the environment. It is awareness that provides real information about the needs of the organism, promotes self-regulation, and coordinates the balance between the inner world and the environment. Awareness is a basic concept in Gestalt Therapy.

I remember that in those days, the topic of psycho-pathology, in the context of the Gestalt approach, was an unexplored territory and it could only "boast" about few articles and small chapters in monographs by some well-known psychotherapists. The Gestalt methodology of working with various mental sufferings was passed on by word of mouth at advanced training seminars; it had been developed by those professionals who, working in the field of mental health, were creating an original clinical Gestalt based on their practical empirical experience.

I was very inspired by this example of my colleagues and respected mentors and I dared to describe my psychotherapeutic experience in supporting people with mental disorders in a methodological academic book.

The idea to write the book was fueled by the deep interest I had in the mental world of those who literally feel what is happening in the environment in a different way or those who do not deny reality but do not want to know anything about it and run away from it into neurotic perception or into the "bodily madness" of conversion disorder.

I would like to note that working with people with mental disorders in the Gestalt Therapy paradigm not only helped me to step away from the one-sided norm-centered expert position of a clinical psychologist, but also to complete it with a commitment to existential dialogue, as well as the ability to experimentally seek new ways of creative adjustment for each individual client and for myself in this process. In addition, it highlighted my own "dark" spots, and helped me to feel that in humanistic psychotherapy, a specialist firstly is a personality, and only then he or she is a professional.

But years passed... From time to time I worked enthusiastically on the book, adding new chapters and rewriting the previous ones; periodically I put it aside for quite a long time and was absorbed exclusively in private practice, conducting educational and social projects in psychotherapy. A few years ago, I left my job as a psychologist in a public hospital and in a private outpatient medical center, but people suffering from phobias, panic attacks, conversion syndromes, or personality disorders continued to come to my psychotherapy office regularly and they still do it. This fact led me to the conclusion that my work with mental disorders has never stopped and is unlikely to disappear from my professional life. And, now, after 15 years of active practice of clinical Gestalt Therapy, I am ready to publish a book that describes some ideas and visions of working with certain forms of mental pathologies.

I consider that methodologization of psychotherapy of mental disorders in the Gestalt paradigm is of great practical and theoretical importance for interdisciplinary cooperation of Gestalt-oriented clinical psychologists, psychiatrists, and representatives of other psychotherapeutic approaches and related specialties.

This book will hopefully be of interest to the psychotherapeutic community, encouraging mental health specialists and personal development professionals to engage in discussion and dialogue that will create fruitful ground for therapists and their clients.

All cases of psychotherapeutic work provided in the book were written by the permission of the clients, and in some places some information was intentionally changed to preserve confidentiality.

ACKNOWLEDGMENTS

The publication of this book would not have been possible without the participation of a large number of people who have been contributing individually over the years to support the writing of the manuscript. I am filled with deep gratitude to all of them.

I express my special gratitude to the sagacious psychiatrist, wonderful person and my loyal friend Nataliya Lapa - I will always remember her deep and systematic psychopathological analyses during my time at the hospital, her collegial advice, sensitive support and all the extremely important clinical lessons I learned from her.

I would also like to express my gratitude to my Ukrainian colleagues - Maryna Stepanchenko, Oleksandra Odehova, Olena Lysenko, Mahdalyna Pakholok, Kateryna Balakirieva, Tetiana Selyukova, Natalia Zlyhostieva, and Valeriia Bykova - who read the initial and draft versions of the book chapters, gave honest constructive criticism, and shared their support with me.

I would like to express my sincere gratitude to Olena Khavkina for her exceptional work in bringing this book to a new audience.

I am deeply grateful for the invaluable help of Molly Rawle, whose dedication to advancing authentic Gestalt Therapy through Gestalt Journal Press and her support have been pivotal in preparing this manuscript for publication. Her wisdom, honesty, and kindness have been a guiding light for me, and I am sincerely thankful for her contribution.

And, of course, this book would never have been completed without the support and enthusiasm of so many wonderful Gestalt students who frustrated my interruptions in writing the book and kept me going. I will never forget their support, as the result of their efforts is now on paper. I thank them for their interest and for waiting for this manuscript.

I am grateful to all my patients and clients - young children, teenagers, adults, couples and families - for trusting me and choosing me as their therapist; I have learned a lot from all of them and I am carrying this knowledge and experience further into Life.

INTRODUCTION
TO CLINICAL GESTALT THERAPY

In recent decades, mental disorders have become a particularly pressing acute problem for psychiatrists and clinical psychologists who practice humanistic psychotherapy methods, including the Gestalt approach. The development of a new biopsychosocial health paradigm, replacing the biomedical model that had more than a 300-year tradition, has facilitated the introduction of these psychotherapeutic approaches into the structure of medical institutions and the psychosocial counseling sector.

Gestalt Therapy, with its view of the holism of the biological, psychological and social in human life, with its emphasis on phenomenology, on the recognition the uniqueness and originality of each individual personality, is a very promising psychotherapeutic direction for the treatment of various psychopathological disorders, fitting organically into the concepts of the new general medical paradigm. Commitment to the idea of holism distinguishes Gestalt Therapy from other psychotherapeutic approaches that emphasize either the expansion of behavioral repertoire to improve adaptive interaction between a person and society (behavioral psychotherapy) or the rational rethinking of fragments of old life experiences, believing that this can change a person's life in the future (psychoanalysis).

So far, attempts to introduce Gestalt Therapy into the practice of clinical institutions for psychotherapeutic support of patients with various pathologies and efforts to integrate the approaches of traditional psychiatry and Gestalt have been made by specialists from different countries worldwide; they are reflected in the publications by Van Baalen (2010), Ginger (1995), Greenberg (2016), Melnick & Nevis (1992; 1997), Harris (1992), Taylor (2014), Spagnuolo Lobb (2002; 2018), Francesetti (2015), Roubal (2007) and many other authors (Carlock, Glaus, Shaw, 1992; Pintus, 2017; Schulthess, 2006; Yontef, 1988; 1993; 2001). In addition to publications, the number of training programs - specializations initiated by Gestalt institutes on the use of the approach in the field of psychopathology has increased significantly.

It is important to emphasize that the issue of developing effective support for people suffering from various disorders concerns not only the use of the Gestalt approach in clinical activities by Gestalt practitioners who work on a regular basis in the health care system. Gestalt therapists who are engaged in private practice of providing psychological assistance often deal with clients who bring problems of their own symptomatology too. These range from rare episodes of acute anxiety and psychosomatic reactions to severe depressive disorders and psychotic states. These professionals have to face the challenge of how they can be most useful to such specific, disorganized people, given that in the format of a private consultation they have more professional limits, for example, they cannot monitor the behavior of a person suffering from psychosis after a psychotherapeutic intervention session, leaving them under the care of colleagues and nurses, which, on the contrary, is possible for Gestalt therapists working in medicine.

The purpose of this book is to support and strengthen the trend of integrating the Gestalt approach into psychotherapeutic work with people with mental disorders. The book provides examples of the ideas of author's colleagues and his own attempts to translate the terms of psychopathology into the language in order to enrich both approaches with the novelty that is so necessary for the growth and with strengthening of the professional interest of Gestalt therapists in clinical psychotherapy. The relevance of understanding psychopathological disorders from the perspective of the Gestalt approach, as well as the need to develop adaptive strategies for psychotherapy of people suffering from these disorders, is undoubted. It opens the door to a new space of awareness, experimentation, research, and co-creation that we can explore together with our colleagues and our clients - fellow travelers who are looking for new boundaries of existence and new ways to live in this difficult and ever-changing world.

NOTES ON THE TERMS USED

The theory and practice of Gestalt Therapy is based on the principle of holism - i.e., integrity; however, within the area itself there is no unity in the use and definition of certain concepts; there are different methodological interpretations and diametrically opposed points of view. We can see this difference in the postulates of individual schools and institutes of Gestalt Therapy that are scattered around the world, as well as read about it in monographs by individual authors or hear it at training seminars.

As the readers may have studied in different programs with excellent Gestalt trainers who may have spoken the same language but with different dialects, I would like to clarify some of the terms that will be used in this book.

First of all, this concerns the issue of resistance. [2] Resistance in the Gestalt paradigm is also called disruptions of the contact cycle, mechanisms of contact interruption, neurotic defense mechanisms, etc. Fritz Perls used the term "resistance" in his first book *Ego, Hunger and Aggression* (1947) and described work with various types of interruptions of contact between the Organism and the environment. Later, this very term was adopted by some Gestalt institutes.

----

[2] Resistance is a fundamental concept in Gestalt Therapy. The task of the Gestalt therapist is to identify "resistances" that oppose the free flow of the contact cycle or the cycle of need satisfaction or self-realization. The main types of resistance are: confluence, introjection, projection, retroreflection, deflection, egotism, and invalidation (Ginger, 1995).

The next important point concerns whether this or that resistance is something that interrupts contact[3] or, on the contrary, organizes it. This conceptual issue has been discussed by European Gestalt therapists for decades (Ginger & Ginger, 1987; Francesetti, Gecele, Roubal, 2013). My position on it is as follows: initially, what I call resistance was a way of creative adjustment, a normal pattern of behavior that became a disruption of the contact cycle when it was used systematically unconsciously, in an anachronistic inflexible way, and it is what disrupts the present homeostasis.[4]

Let's take projection[5] as an example. It is projection that initially helps us to build an empathic bridge with another human being, it is our subjective, "understanding", "sensitive" vision, and the proven shortcut by which the lived experience of the past enters the territory of the present. However, our use of projection without emphasis on personal responsibility and receptivity to new data of the situation and environment leads to a distortion of reality and prevents a person from assessing their contribution to the interaction with the environment.

---

3. Contact is the process of energy exchange between a person and the environment, in which the necessary is received from the environment and the unnecessary is rejected.

4. Homeostasis is the relative dynamic stability of the internal environment of the body, which is maintained at several levels: both at the cellular and molecular levels of individual organs, and at the level of the whole organism in the form of human behavior in the environment. Gestalt therapists emphasize that homeostasis is a dynamic balance of the human body in the environment, and its violation can lead to certain suffering.

5. Projection is a classic form of resistance, that consists in attributing one's own feelings, emotions, thoughts, and problems to other people.

There is one more aspect is the naming of certain resistances. In the text, I use the term Confluence 1 and it may not be familiar to all Gestalt therapists, as it is traditionally used mainly by the French specialist Salathé (1988) and followers of the experimental direction of Gestalt Therapy (Ginger, 1995). What is this mechanism of contact interruption? Confluence 1 is resistance in which a significant figure does not stand out from the background or is misidentified. Confluence 1 also prevents a person from becoming aware of their needs and can protect them from pain. In other areas of our approach, mainly in Gestalt institutes in the United States and the United Kingdom, the confluence 1 is called desensitization, but the essence and phenomenological characteristics of this resistance remain identical (Joyce & Sills, 2001). In contrast to confluence 1, confluence 2 is resistance in which the other person's figure is perceived as one's own, and the person is not guided by his or her own needs and desires when organizing contact.

I also want to be honest and say that the book is written at the intersection of traditional medical and psychotherapeutic approaches and is replete with many medicalisms. The reader will come across such words as "conversion", "nosogeny", "amnesia,"[6] and many others in the text. I have certainly considered simplifying the psychiatric vocabulary in favor of the phenomenological language that is more common in Gestalt Therapy, but I was still inclined to the idea that this manuscript can enrich both professional languages with new meanings and tried to find some balance.

[6.] Amnesia is the absence of memory, the loss of the ability to store and reproduce previously acquired knowledge and experience.

NOTES ON THE IDEA OF PSYCHOPATHOLOGY
IN GESTALT

The view of psychopathology is even more controversial and acute than the issue discussed above regarding the terms used in Gestalt Therapy.

I would suggest that there are three approaches to understanding clinical problems among professionals in our community, but I assume that there may be more - perhaps as many as the number of Gestalt therapists.

The first approach is ultra-phenomenological and proclaims that there is no such thing as a mental disorder (nor is there a somatic disease). Proponents of this view sometimes vigorously argue for the paramount necessity of researching the phenomena experienced, as opposed to various concepts - including psychiatric, psychodynamic, and cognitive - that attempt to understand the nature and characterization of mental suffering and its various symptoms. Thus, since Gestalt therapists work first of all with the client's subjectivity, even if their experience is, say, hypochondriacal and contradicts the objective data of medical examinations and analyzes, it makes no practical sense for a specialist to use the concept of "hypochondria" in this case, because it does not correspond to the personality of the person presented to the world around them. At this point, subjectivity is identified with one-sidedness, and the ultra-phenomenological approach itself is increasingly similar to an anti-psychiatric slogan that breaks ties with related professionals from the medical environment.

The second approach is an attempt to create an autonomous Gestalt psychopathology based mainly on the Self[7] theory of Paul Goodman and Isadore From and the current field paradigm in Gestalt Therapy. This direction also emphasizes phenomenological philosophy, but without being radical. Followers of this approach "are not guided by the question: 'Does the subject suffer?' but rather the question 'Does the relationship suffer?" (Francesetti, Gecele, Roubal, 2013).

Psychopathological suffering, perceived by a person, develops in relationships and is a characteristic of contact boundary.[8]

---

7. Self — in the theory of Gestalt Therapy, this word does not denote / refer to a separate entity (which can be said about the "I" in psychoanalysis), but a certain process consisting of a set of manifestations of a person at the interface between the organism and the environment, which allows for creative adjustment. Creative adjustment is a mode of conscious behavior associated with making a decision to change oneself or the environment. In contrast to creative adjustment, there is conservative adjustment, which is unconscious behavior with the preservation of habitual patterns of relationships. Self has three functions: Id (associated with internal impulses, vital needs and their bodily manifestation), Personality (associated with the integration of experience, the formation of one's own identity and self-concept) and Ego (representing the active ability to make responsible choices while being aware of one's own needs and the context of the environment) (Ginger, 1995).

8. Contact boundary is a fundamental concept in classical and modern Gestalt Therapy. It is believed that psychotherapy takes place at the boundary-contact between the client and their environment (in particular, the therapist): it is here that contact resistances can be detected / identify and the normal cycle of need satisfaction can take place (Ginger, 1995).

This view tries to consider a variant of creative adjustment in each mental disorder, and in this context, the Gestalt therapist, relying on creativity, looks for new opportunities for adjustment together with a client. In recent decades, this approach has been actively developed by Franchised, Spagnuolo Lobb, Gecele, Salonia and Rubal and it undoubtedly enriches Gestalt methodology in working with clients with various clinical problems (Franchised, Gecele, Roubal, 2013; Franchised, 2015; Roubal, 2007). However, I would like to note the need for preliminary scientific research with further validation of our method in this area and the risk of separating Gestalt therapists from psychiatrists and psychothera-pists of other modalities due to the use of different terms for the same mental processes. I would like Gestalt therapists in their development of this approach, following the idea of Ginger (1995), to avoid the temptation and fantasy of paranoid omnipotence, which pushes any specialist to the desire to "re-create the world".

The third view of psychopathology is based on the canonical experimental paradigm and the integrative possibilities of Gestalt Therapy together with other psychotherapeutic approaches. Proponents of this direction focus their work on the study of the peculiarities of the boundary between a client and the environment, or rather on the mechanisms of contact interruption that disrupt this contact interaction, creating various symptom formation. Psychotherapy must include experimental forms of work, which are designed to expand the client's awareness and behavioral reper-toire, as well as to provide a person with the opportunity to gain new experiences. The formation of disorders is caused by the mechanisms of interruption in various modalities of bound-ary-contact, the accumulation of a certain amount of "unclosed gestalts", i. e. interrupted or unmet needs and avoided relationships with the environment, which can eventually be transformed into certain clinical symptoms. The third approach openly and boldly integrates the existential-phenomenological basis of Gestalt

Therapy with psychodynamic, neo-Reichian and behaviorist directions, respecting, for example, the contribution of such specialists as Nancy McWilliams, Otto Kernberg, Carl Gustav Jung, Donald Woods Winnicott, and not neglecting the contribution of modern traditional psychiatry and recent developments in the field of neuroscience (Ginger, 1995). The focus on interdisciplinary cooperation with psychiatric and somatic physicians, the achievement of consensus in the use of nosological categories, and the attempt to build bridges between the use of psychopathology and Gestalt concepts are what distinguish this third position towards the problem of clinical suffering. A significant contribution to the development of this approach was made by Ginger and Ginger (1987; 2008), Melnick and Nevis (1992; 1997), and Elinor Greenberg (2016). In my book, I adhere to and continue to develop the understanding of the acute issue of Gestalt psychopathology in this very context.

Years of traveling the path of clinical Gestalt Therapy have led me to some conclusions and reference points that I will share here.

1. Moving away from the nosology and focusing only on the changing moments of the current process can lead to a misguided personalized intervention from the psychotherapist. I am close to the important remarks of Melnick and Nevis (1992) that clients who are hopeless from the point of view of a traditional diagnosis are not so obviously hopeless in the light of the "here and now" approach and Gestalt therapists may not assess the degree of the patient's isolation within their pathological behavior, the persistence of their disorders, thus causing a psychotherapeutic mistake in the future [Melnick & Nevis, 1992].

2. I believe that Gestalt Therapy in the context of hospital treatment of somatic and mental disorders requires some modification. It is worth noting that the most important reason for the

success of Gestalt Therapy in work with people suffering from various pathologies is diligent work on awareness. Those patients who want to get rid of their clinical symptoms without such work are the category that prefers more medication-based psychotropic treatment and behavioral psychotherapy. At the same time, the use of psychopharmacological support at the initial and more advanced stages of psychotherapy is, in some cases, not rare, and a necessary condition for the management of patients suffering from severe mental disorders.

3. I am convinced that when psychotherapy succeeds in handling the client's neurotic misery or "dissolving" their chronic psychosomatic syndrome, psychological assistance is not over - the work will now be aimed at getting out of the human misery, towards the existential data and improving the life quality.

4. In my opinion, when working with clients with clinical problems, a Gestalt therapist needs to rely on a certain expert knowledge of understanding the picture of mental disorders, while recognizing the uniqueness of each individual case. It is important for a specialist to be able to build a therapeutic dialogic relationship with a client, to be aware of what kind of experiments are appropriate and accessible to a suffering person and what are not, and to recognize their professional limits in this area of practice.

5. People suffering from psychopathology refuse to be aware of the present, refuse to be spontaneous, refuse to be truly close and honest with themselves and the world around them; they do not recognize their needs, are unable to organize them into a hierarchy or cannot satisfy them; such people are constrained by a pessimistic picture of their lives, falling into one of the categories of the mental disorders classification. Gestalt Therapy does not offer a universal solution to this problem for society and humanity as a whole, but it gives hope and offers to improve the life for each individual by clarifying the role of feelings, physicality, and

experiences in the "here and now", gaining new experiences and completing gestalts related to the past.

6. An attractive feature of Gestalt Therapy in working with people with mental disorders is the ability to open up a wide range of human uniqueness and allow them to take from it what they need and what distinguishes them, rather than leading these clients to some general conceptual norm of what healthy people should be like in order to be considered "cured".

When *Gestalt Therapy: Excitement and Growth in the Human Personality* was first introduced, Fritz Perls, Paul Goodman, and Ralph Hefferline (1951) emphasized the importance of this idea, which remains relevant today. The authors emphasized that if the basic concept of a healthy human character is true, all people cured of neurotic disorders would become similar, but is this really the case? In their opinion, it is more likely that, having reached health and spontaneity, people begin to be different, unique and original, but people with a certain type of neurosis are similar, because the "deadening" effect of their disorder is evident.

Now that we have dealt with the general principles of clinical Gestalt Therapy, we can move on to the following chapters to study specific examples of mental suffering and how to work with it.

CHAPTER 1

GESTALT APPROACH
TO WORK WITH NOSOGENIES
IN CHILDREN AND ADOLESCENTS

Nosogenies are a group of mental disorders that are usually formed in response to a clinical diagnosis made by doctors in the presence of a serious somatic disease (malignant oncopathological neoplasms, insulin-dependent diabetes mellitus, myocardial infarction). It is the semantic significance of the diagnosis, the life-threatening danger, which is associated with by a sick person, and the awareness of a threat to one's existence due to the onset of a serious illness that is a factor of specific psychosocial stress that causes nosogenia, while the factor of the impact of somatic harm on the course of a mental disorder is secondary. According to the results of clinical studies, nosogenies are much more frequent than other mental disorders observed in general medical practice (Fitkalko, Filts, Lizak, Bozhenko, 2022).

According to my observations, in some cases, nosogeny can become of such a strong and maladaptive nature that psychotherapeutic intervention to reduce it is no less important in the first stages of therapy than direct treatment of the underlying somatic disease. Nosogenies are generally disorders of a neurotic level of response and therefore they are reversible disorders, but working with them practically is far from being an easy task for clinical psychologists and psychotherapists.

This chapter is devoted to the consideration of nosogenies in children and adolescents from the perspective of Gestalt Therapy. Here, I have attempted to translate the clinical picture from the terms of psychiatry into the methodological language of our approach, and to highlight possible strategies for a psychotherapist working with this category of disorders, since this issue, as far as I know, is not covered at all in the classical and modern Gestalt literature.

Most of the patients suffering from nosogenies with whom I worked in a general somatic hospital were adolescents, and therefore I will pay more attention to them in my presentation of the material.

In different schools of psychiatry, nosogenies have many names - "personality reaction to the disease", "disease consciousness", "disease experience", but in the latest version of ICD-10 and in the new ICD-11 version, which is currently being finalized, they do not have their own terms. At the same time, from the point of view of various psychiatrists, relatively short-term nosogenies with anxiety-phobic and mild depressive syndromes can be classified as adaptation disorders in ICD-10.

Psychiatry has developed several typologies of nosogenies, which for convenience, can be divided into reactions that reflect the high significance of a somatic disease - they are divided into anxiety-phobic, depressive, hypochondriacal, sensitive, obsessive-compulsive, paranoid, as well as reactions of underestimating the significance of the disease in the form of pathological denial of the disease and a state of "beautiful indifference".

Based on our clinical experience, anxiety, sensitivity, and depressive reactions prevail among adolescents suffering from severe endocrinological and oncohematological diseases, and anxiety-phobic, anosognosic, and paranoid nosogenies are less common.

Anxiety nosogenies in adolescents are characterized by an almost constant concern about possible severe complications of their disease, its lethal and tragic outcome, and the ineffectiveness of the somatic treatment methods used. The mood of these adolescents is characterized by a predominance of anxiety, and they also have symptoms of a vegetative nature, such as heart palpitations, headaches, dizziness, and breathing difficulties. Anxiety can be accompanied by specific fears, such as the fear of children with cancer dying during surgery.

> *For example, 12-year-old Katya fought bravely to overcome lymphogranulomatosis, but for the past few months she has been experiencing an obsessive fear of being alone in a room, always accompanied by an attack of heart palpitations, dizziness and difficulty breathing. During the first psychotherapy sessions, when she told me about this fear, she said that she was not able to identify what exactly she was afraid of when she was alone in a room, "I'm very scared; something bad is going to happen; it becomes difficult for me to breathe".*

Adolescents with depressive reactions can rarely focus on current experiences; their judgments are directed to the future and this future is seen by them as extremely pessimistic, the results of treatment are seen as negative, even if doctors give them favorable objective data from medical examinations. They express suicidal thoughts out loud, and they interpret possible complications of the disease as an approaching death. Here is a clinical example of such nosogeny.

A 17-year-old, Valeriy, a strong, athletic, tall, bald after chemotherapy, and his mother, a modest, friendly woman, came to the consultation. Valeriy has a relapse of acute lymphoblastic leukemia a couple of months after having been discharged from the hospital. Before his illness, the boy had a strong-willed character, he was a candidate for master of sports in Greco-Roman wrestling, and wanted to enter a military academy. Now he has a chronic depressed mood; he lost interest in life, in things that used to excite him, and he says he "wants to jump out of the window rather than wait for the next 'chemotherapy' because the result will be death anyway". He refuses to undergo medical treatment. His mother is unable to instil in him any hope for the success of treatment and is very worried. During the consultation, he is sitting hunched over, looking at the floor, with an alienated, sad face; his mother is sitting next to him and looks at me and then at him.

T: Valera, you've been sitting hunched over and looking at the floor for a few minutes now. Should we try to talk?

C: Why should we? There is no point in it. I'm going to die anyway, it's all over anyway.

T: When you said those words, your mother had tears in her eyes. How do you think your mother might feel hearing something like that?

C: I don't care how she feels anymore. I don't care what she says. Everything is over. I'm going to die of this damn leukemia and it better happen soon.

In case of sensitive nosogenies, adolescents are full of worries that someone around them (classmates, friends, teachers) may form an unfavorable impression of them due to the fact that they have a certain disease. They fantasize that their acquaintances will avoid communicating with them, stop respecting them, and treat them with pity, contempt, and disgust, as "lepers or inferior individuals". The sad thing is that sometimes the family and friends react in this very way, thus implementing the phenomenon of self-fulfilling prophecy, causing social stigmatization of young people, and this increases their sensitive fears. For example, very often adolescents suffering from insulin-dependent diabetes mellitus hide their disease from classmates or friends, because in the teenage subculture, which lacks the necessary education about diseases, this disease is often shamefully compared to drug addiction, which in itself hurts and stigmatizes children.

With paranoid reactions to illness, adolescents are convinced that their illness is the result of malicious intent, that possible complications and side effects of medications are the result of negligence, lack of proper qualifications of doctors or nurses, "who really don't care about their suffering, because unless you give them money, they won't do anything sensible at all".

Clinicians agree that nosogenies are formed under the influence of such factors as premorbid personality traits of the patient, the nature of the somatic disease itself, and the attitude to this disease in the microsocial community, which is especially significant for the patient. At the same time, nosogenies are formed differently in a child than in an adult. To a large extent, a child's reaction to his or her illness is affected by being placed in a hospital, being with other patients, limiting activity, and being separated from classmates, friends, and family members. Understanding of the disease in children and adolescents is more represented at the emotional and sensory (unconscious) level than at the level of logical understanding (conscious). The reasons for incomplete awareness may include lack of awareness, childishly naive knowledge that distorts the true understanding of the disease, insufficient maturity of intellectual and mental functions, and peculiarities of psychological defense mechanisms.

INTROJECTS AND DISEASES

Translating the language of clinical psychiatry into the language of resistance adopted in Gestalt, it should be noted that nosogeny in a sick person is based on thoughts and attitudes about their illness that were previously introduced by them from the outside world. In the Gestalt approach, a pathological introject is a fragment of someone else's experience, a part of the environment inside a person that has penetrated the body without prior comprehension and living and is currently a factor poisoning their existence, their relationships with themselves and with others.

Considering the role of introjection in the onset of nosogeny, it is worth noting that introjection is an integral process of socialization and upbringing of a child; it is with its help that a child absorbs language, norms, values, guidelines for how to interact with the environment, and therefore with its help they try to understand the situation of change in their existence - the situation of disease. The information about the disease is introduced from those figures with whom the sick child is in a state of confluence 2, most of these are parents, doctors and medical staff, as well as some other sick children and parents who care for them. The child conflows with the environment, with the transition from "I" to "we", because it reduces emotional stress, and the child does not feel lonely, helpless, and hopeless in the situation of illness. With the help of confluence, the child feels safe. The unconscious desire for the confluence 2 can be initiated not only by the children themselves, but also by their parents, who are overwhelmed by fear and stress, because their child has diabetes or acute leukemia and may die, leaving them forever.

For a child, the most emotionally significant are the beliefs and thoughts about the disease that they internalized from their parents, as they are used to believing in their exceptional rightness without criticism from the first years of their life. It is to the parents that the child reports his or her first somatic complaints, and they take him or her to the clinic or call a doctor in, discuss the dynamics of the disease, perform home medical procedures, give pills, ointments, drops, and sometimes injections. The family's perception of the disease, the level of education and medical culture largely determines how the child will treat the disease. In cases of nosogenies in adolescents and young children, introjections are maladaptive, distorting the true cause and prognosis of the disease, complicating relationships with doctors, demotivating treatment, tearing the child's inner world apart, and sometimes driving them crazy.

As an illustration, let me tell you a story of 12-year-old Bohdan. When psychotherapy started, he had been suffering from insulin-dependent diabetes for two years and a half and showed signs of high emotional instability. The boy had an extremely negative attitude towards his illness. He was hostile to doctors, did not want to take the necessary doses of insulin; anxiety and anger were his dominant features. During one of the consultations, a belief introduced by his mother about his diabetes was revealed: "These doctors have made you a drug addict. Now you have to take these injections all your life, and you can't get away from it. But everything could have been different if we hadn't given the doctors the permission to take insulin, if we hadn't believed them that this was a disease that could only be treated with insulin injections, if we had taken you to a healer and he would have cured you". Soon after, I met with Bohdan's mother to discuss this maladaptive view of the disease, and she confirmed to me that these were her words, which she was not going to retract because she was convinced that they were true. Unfortunately, this case is far from rare in the clinic of nosogenies in adolescents with diabetes.

It is also worth noting that the process of introjecting catastrophic or maladaptive beliefs about the disease observed in nosogeny can be initiated not only by one of the patient's relatives, but also by the patient's doctor. The cause of the disorder is the doctor's misconduct in the form of careless statements about the severity and bad prognosis of the disease, allowing the sick child to read medical records, telling the child about the poor outcome of a similar disease in another patient, intimidating the child so that they better understands the need to follow certain treatment rules. This iatrogenic effect is often beyond the doctor's awareness; it can be observed in interns or young specialists who have just started practice, as well as in "experienced" doctors who show signs of professional burnout and neuroticism and in those who consider this way of interacting with a child to be the most adequate and appropriate for the treatment situation.

Children introject the thoughts and view of doctors without critical processing, because it is the doctor who is the key figure accompanying them in the situation of disease - a doctor relieves somatic pain by prescribing appropriate procedures, which reduces anxiety, fear, despair in children giving them a sense of security. It is the doctor who provides initial information about the specifics of the disease, the need for ongoing treatment, nutrition regulation, and possible consequences in case of violation of the regimen. This is especially important for children, both in case of somatic crisis conditions with rapid progression of the disease (acute leukemia, Burkitt's lymphoma) and in case when the disease is chronic and can lead to gradual complications and disability in the future (diabetes mellitus, bronchial asthma). The child introjects thoughts, attitudes, and values not only of the objects of their love, but also of objects towards which they feel dissatisfaction, anger, and which have power over them, while the doctor has the prerogative of power and the ability to influence the young patient and can cause ambivalent feelings.

In some cases, the entire environment of an inpatient hospital ward is a translator of pathological introjections. A little child with his or her mother or a teenager, when admitted to such a ward, from the very first minutes of their stay, are carefully "fed" by other patients or their parents, and sometimes this information can be simply horrifying. For example, in the case of diabetes: *"With such sugar levels, it is not known whether you will live to see the morning"* or *"In this department you will not be helped properly; the doctors here do not know how to treat diabetes, you need to go to Kyiv - there is a chance there"*. In case of cancer: *"With a diagnosis like yours, three children have already died here, so hold on, hold on"*. The "feeding" of introjects in such wards is mutual among children and adults, resembling a "mutual responsibility", and it is extremely difficult for a psycho-therapist working with nosogenic patients from such a ward to work with them, as he or she sometimes opposes, indirectly or directly, such a pathologizing environment.

In some cases, introjections about the disease lead to the gradual growth of neuroticism and can be received by patients several years before the formation of the actual nosogeny. In other cases, introjections act quickly, like a poison, affecting a child or adolescent with a neurotic disorder in a short time.

The introjections that cause nosogeny vary in content, but they mainly relate to understanding the onset of a somatic disease, its prognosis, and the attitude of people around it in society.

It is important to distinguish several groups of introjections that deal with the onset of a serious somatic disease among adolescents:

1. Magical introjections.
2. Introjections of religious origin.
3. Psychotherapeutic introjections.

Magical introjections. Somatically ill adolescents are characterized by the following introjective understanding of their illness: "Your disease arose because someone put a spell on you, jinxed you, cursed you, your family, your lineage".

Here's an example.

Victoria, who was diagnosed with insulin-dependent diabetes at the age of 15, was convinced that her disease was caused by a curse. There was a tense emotional climate in the girl's family - her paternal grandmother was against the marriage of her father and mother and tried to separate them in every possible way, building various plots over the years. Six months before the onset of diabetes, her grandmother would come to their house and throw soil from the cemetery under the carpet, cursing her mother and granddaughter openly, reproaching them for "taking her son away from her, and he was supposed to live with her, to take care of her mother in her difficult old age". When the girl was diagnosed with diabetes, her mother instilled in her with the idea that the disease was the result of her grandmother's magic curse. The patient experienced neurotic guilt for not being able to prevent her disease, "because she did not seek help in time from people who have some psychic abilities, and it was possible, but it was always put off".

In rare cases, adolescents swallow their parents' introjects that their somatic illness is of **bioenergetic origin**: "I got diabetes because of energy vampires - people who suck my life out, take my energy, for example, my envious schoolmates".

Introjects of religious origin. Introjects that are more common in Christianity are "I got this disease because of my sins" or "I atone for my parents' sins". In the first case, children drown in painful fantasies about what sins they have committed that God has punished them so, and experience an illusory sense of guilt, and in the second case, they reward / give / "reward" their parents with negative projections, have ambivalent feelings or feelings of hatred and resentment toward them. In some cases, these feelings are not expressed out loud, but are retroflected[9], which increases children's emotional suffering.

Psychotherapeutic introjects. Introjects of this group also have a place in the structure of resistance, although they are quite rare. They are mostly based on the interpretations of specialists that adolescents receive during psychological counseling. These introjects are often not learned by patients from highly qualified psychotherapists, who are more focused on supporting and building strong therapeutic relationships with children and know that interpretation requires timeliness and relevance. Most often, patients receive such kind of introjects from interns who are doing their training in a hospital and want to figure things out quickly and cure the patient within one session, and from specialists who do not have the necessary many years of psychoanalytic education and, in fact, do not practice psychotherapy professionally.

---

[9] **Retroflection** is another of the resistances, which is the tendency to turn the mobilized energy to the detriment of oneself (e. g., somatization) or to do to oneself what one would like to get from others.

If we are talking about introjects related to the prognosis of the disease, they depend on its nosology and are quite variable. In the case of diabetes, these are introjections that a miracle treatment will soon be found that will cure the disease forever; or these can be various introjections about a slow death with severe somatic complications, and it is in the second case that adolescents, demonstrating a counterpoint to the introvertive message, prefer to achieve a lethal outcome as soon as possible by systematically disrupting their diet and insulin intake.

Anxious fantasies, sensitive fears, catastrophic expectations about the reaction of society to the fact of illness, unfounded beliefs that other people are to be blamed and involved in the onset of somatic disease, which are observed in different variants of nosogeny in adolescents, are projections of one's own feelings and wishes into the external environment, and hypothetically, one's own rejected parts can live in these projective phenomenon. These projections are also based on earlier introjections from such somatically ill people or from family members.

PSYCHOTHERAPEUTIC STRATEGY FOR DEALING WITH NOSOGENIES

The psychotherapist works with the resistance that is identified at the beginning of the therapy session, but at the same time keeps in mind other remittances that cause nosogeny. Usually, such a "façade" resistance of the patient, which first comes into the focus of the specialist's attention, is a retroreflection of their own experiences in the modality of thinking - "I think about my illness all the time, these annoying thoughts do not allow me to live normally, to sleep peacefully; it's like an annoying song that is always playing in my head and from which I am so tired". Or, at the beginning of psychotherapy, it can be the patient's projections of alienation, which are typical for sensitive nosogenies - "people around me will avoid me because of my illness when I am discharged from the hospital". A careful study of these projections and retroflections in the traditional Gestalt mode leads the psychotherapist to the patient's introjections about the nature, prognosis, and attitude of the environment towards the disease, and to those figures who transmitted these messages and with whom the patient was in a situation of merging at the time of introjection.

I would like to focus special attention on working with the inrojects that cause nosogeny. It is important for the psychotherapist to help the adolescent to identify the introjected message that can be experienced as his or her own thoughts, to clarify in what situations these messages are actualized, and to try to verbalise them, to give them an appropriate voice, timbre, and intonation that helps to establish the source of the introject. Often the introject is accepted by an adolescent or child in a state far from conscious, filled with feelings of hopelessness and fear, and in psychotherapeutic work it is important that this introject is heard anew and comprehended in a conscious mode. It is necessary to clarify the patient's feelings towards the figures who transmitted the introjected message and to understand with what feelings this message was transmitted to the patient, because sometimes the message may seem very harsh, but was transmitted by parents out of fear, their own shame or helplessness.

British Gestalt therapists Joyce & Sills (2001) recommend strategies for working with introjects that can also be used in psychotherapy of nosogenies. They believe that sometimes role-playing is useful, which can give the adolescent the opportunity to return to the situation when they took the introject. The adolescent can try to make a different decision, reject the introject, change it, or, based on their own experience and resources, argue with the person who sends the introject, or confront him or her. You can try to find an introject with the patient that is opposite in content - recall a particularly respected person who may be guided by completely opposite views on the problem of the disease.

For example, in the course of psychotherapy with 14-year-old Oleksandra, it became clear that her anxious and depressed mood, which had been observed for a year, was associated with frequent thoughts about the terrible complications of diabetes. She was convinced that she would soon lose a kidney, despite the fact that her glyceria control was optimal and no complications were identified, according to medical examinations. Oleksandra did not tell anyone about her feelings, she kept them to herself (retroflected), closing more and more inside her pathological behavior. It turned out that she had internalized this attitude about the loss of a kidney after a conversation a year ago with her local doctor, who was not an endocrinologist by specialization. In the situation of introjecting, Oleksandra had problems with high blood sugar, which were not clear at the time, despite following dietary therapy and taking insulin regularly, and she, being a vulnerable girl with a sensitive personality, was very worried about it. The district doctor, who came to her house, was in a bad mood, shouted at her and her mother without any reason and said that with "such an attitude to diabetes treatment, you will lose your kidneys in two years". For a year, the girl was immersed in the process of neurotization, in the worry that she would soon lose her kidney, which eventually caused nosogenia. Appealing to the opposite opinion of her regular endocrinologist, who treated Oleksandra carefully and whom she trusted, made it possible to overcome the primary pathological introject about the loss of a kidney.

When working with the introject, it is important to clarify why a person accepted the message and why they still carry it. Further details of Oleksandra's case demonstrate how clarifying these things leads to a situation of incomplete gestalt, the existence of a secondary benefit from accepting such an illusory attitude as the loss of a kidney. Oleksandra's father left her and her mother when she was three years old and had little or no contact with his daughter. The girl lacked communication with her father, missed him very much, and envied her friends who had full families. Her mother never got married again. When the girl got diabetes at the age of nine, her father returned to his former family, took care of her, looked after her, paid a lot of attention, took her to and from school, and Oleksandra was very happy about these changes. But two years later, her father left the family again and began living with another woman who gave birth to his son. The idea of losing a kidney was accepted by the girl because she hoped that if she got such a terrible and severe complication, it would probably bring her father back to the family again, as in the first case with the manifestation of diabetes. The anxiety of losing a kidney was pathologically poisonous, but this possibility was a means of completing the gestalt of having a family together, of being close to the father you love so much and need so much, especially in adolescence, when issues of identity and support from figures who can protect and accept you in your authenticity are so important.

Working with nosogenies in a pediatrics clinic is not only about working exclusively with resistances. It also involves a dialogue with the person seeking help, showing interest in the wider space of his or her life, in addition to the problems surrounding the somatic disease. The patient will have something to tell about themselves, in addition to their diagnosis and when, where, and how they got sick; the factor of selective self-disclosure of the psychotherapist can contribute to new impressions and feelings of the patient, the acquisition of new experiences (the Personality function). Effective work with nosogenies involves immersing a person in critical circumstances, for which it is extremely important to build a strong therapeutic relationship beforehand. In the Gestalt approach, in order to help a patient or client reach this level, the psychotherapist needs to bring his or her own subjectivity to the work, emphasize working in the present moment in direct feelings, and the presence of responsibility for one's choices (Ginger & Ginger, 1987). Without a preliminary building of therapeutic relationships, working with the remittances that organize nosogeny can be equal to a surgical operation without anesthesia, and a person who has experienced such pain may never return to the psychotherapist's office again, especially if he or she is a child or an adolescent.

In conclusion, I would like to note that the use of Gestalt Therapy in the work with children and adolescents suffering from nosogenies not only reduces the effect of neurotic symptoms of this disorder, but also allows to increase the effectiveness of medical treatment of the underlying somatic disease, improve the quality of life of sick people, and also provides a person with the opportunity for a new conscious choice instead of his or her pseudo-choice.

REFERENCES

1. Фіткалько О. С., Фільц О. О., Лизак О. Л., Боженко М. І. (2022). Терапевтичні взаємовідносини при нозогенних реакціях різного типу // Український медичний часопис, 6 (152) – XI/XII, 2022: 59–61.
2. Ginger S., Ginger A. (1987). *La Gestalt, une thérapie du contact. Hommes et Groupes*, Paris.
3. Joyce P. & Sills C. (2001). *Skills in Gestalt Counselling & Psychotherapy*. SAGE Publications Ltd.

CHAPTER 2

PROJECTION
AND DELUSION

"It's not me - it's him / her". This is exactly the kind of phrase that could be on the T-shirts of clients who use projection as the main way of adapting to the world and organize various relationships with other people using the same principle. Projection always shows a tendency to make the environment responsible for the feelings, thoughts, actions, motivations, and values that are born and emerge from the inner world of a person. As a rule, the process of projection in clients is carried out in order to preserve self-respect and avoid unpleasant experiences when facing their own true desires and aspects of their personality that cannot be legally implemented in life due to powerful introjective taboos.

Diagnostic signs that indicate the existence of projections in a client will be a large number of interpretations, assessments, assumptions, judgments about what other people do, thinks, feels, represents, and speculations about why this is happening to them.

For a deeper understanding of the different types of this mechanism, its phenomenological features, strategies and tactics of psychotherapeutic work, readers can refer to the overview of this resistance written by Perls (1947; 1973), Polster & Polster (1973), Ginger & Ginger (1987). My task is to show what role projection plays in the organization of psychopathological suffering and how a psychotherapist can deal with it during a session.

PROJECTION IN THE THERAPEUTIC RELATIONSHIP

A Gestalt therapist strives to help clients become aware of their projections and accept them as their own. When a person gains an honest view of themselves, they can see the difference between themselves and others and no longer be afraid of this difference, to rely on facts rather than distorting interpretations, to experience for the first time the previously alienated properties of sexuality, aggressiveness, creativity, and uniqueness in a completely different way. At the same time, it can be very difficult for a specialist to withstand the competition in the therapeutic relationship imposed by the client through projection, sexual desire in erotic transference[10], and other phenomena of the unified therapist-client psychological field.

Thus, almost every psychotherapist suddenly finds themselves in a situation where they are paying the client back even for something they have never done. It is possible to take directive but promoting interventions out of the pockets of a white coat, an elegant interpretation out of a fashionable psychoanalytic jacket, and sometimes a stunning experiment out of the sleeve of a Gestalt shirt, but at some point, you find yourself dressed in a total and alienating projection.

---

[10] Transference is an intense, emotionally charged attitude of the client to the psychotherapist, which reproduces the client's childhood behavioral pattern to a certain extent.

And a figure of hatred and pain is ignited in the client. And sometimes your arguments, authentic parts of your self that are brought into contact, "empty" chairs and other techniques are powerless in front of this client's projection.

Then you take a chance and say: *"If hating me now makes you hate yourself less, okay, know that I can take it, this is also a part of psychotherapy"*. And this is one example of how a Gestalt therapist, through his or her own controlled self-disclosure, demonstrates a willingness to be resilient to a client's process filled with extremely burdensome feelings and uses frustration to bring a previously unconscious projective behavioral pattern into the zone of awareness.

The prominent Gestalt therapists Ginger & Ginger (1987) also emphasized that in individual therapy, some projective mechanisms can feed the client's transference, and this position is opposed to the counter-psychoanalytic ideas of Fritz Perls about the denial of the mechanism of transference or the possibility of leveling it through a lively dialogue with the client. The authors make an important clarification for practice that if the client attributes to the psychotherapist various qualities that are not peculiar in him or her, endows him or her with great knowledge and omnipotence, the Gestalt therapist, unlike the psychoanalyst, will not cultivate and encourage transfer, but will help the client to be aware of it.

AND NOW ABOUT PROJECTIVE DELUSIONS. . .[11]

Delusions are one of the most severe symptoms that undermine creative adjustment, distort reality, disorganize the thinking process, and are a part of the structure of psychotic disorders.

---

[11] Delusions are a thinking disorder that is a set of morbid ideas, reasoning, and conclusions that take over a person's mind, distort reality, and cannot be corrected by others.

The ideas of delusions are not subject to convincing by the environment, and there is no criticism of them by the psychotic person - on the contrary, he or she demonstrates in every possible way the conviction in the correctness of his or her judgments. Delusional ideas can be very different in content, sometimes grotesquely absurd and dangerous in their consequences.

> *For example, a woman suffering from delusions of jealousy assures others that her husband regularly cheats on her by having sexual contact through the wall in the apartment, and that is why she attacked him at night with a frying pan.*

As a rule, catharsis projections and related introjective prohibitions play a leading role in the structure of jealousy delusions. For example, the introject imposes a strict rule on thoughts about sex and an even stricter prohibition on sexual relations outside of marriage. However, the impulses of libido also do not give up, seek realization and threaten to strike at a person's self-esteem and categorical prohibitions. And then, through the projection of catharsis - resistance, in which the needs, desires, thoughts and actions that a person does not want to recognize in himself or herself are attributed to the outside world - liberation from "grave sexual filth" occurs. Sexual desires and ideas about betrayal are "put" on other people, most often from the inner circle, as described in the example above.

What position should a Gestalt therapist take during a session when their client is in the process of actively forming delusions and moreover, may include the psychotherapist in the plot of his madness? To explain it, I would like to give an example from my own psychotherapeutic practice.

> *A few years ago, I worked with a young girl who had been in a psychotic state for a long time. I worked in tandem with a psychiatrist who regularly monitored the client's condition,*

prescribed and adjusted, if necessary, medication with neuroleptics, and diagnosed her with paranoid schizophrenia[12].

My cooperation with the parents, who initiated a course of psychotherapy for their daughter, also played an important role in this process.

The psychotic process had taken over the girl's personality and held her captive for more than three years before we met. At the beginning of our psychotherapy, her main symptoms were visual and olfactory hallucinations[13] - she smelled burnt human meat, saw otherworldly beings living in her apartment and sometimes trying to play unusual games with her. The client was in social isolation, which was manifested in the fact that she did not attend school and could not contact others. She also had recurrent delusions that she had supernatural powers, which manifested ithemselves in an attempt to revive a pet cat (which had suddenly died) with the help of spells after her father had buried it.

---

[12] Schizophrenia is a severe progressive mental disorder that occurs on the basis of hereditary predisposition, is characterized by the disintegration of mental functions, and is characterized with the obligatory development of a mental defect in the emotional and volitional sphere and various productive psychopathological disorders (delusions, hallucinations, affective disorders, catatonic symptoms, etc.).There are four main forms of schizophrenia: paranoid, simple, catatonic, and hebephrenic ones.

[13.] Hallucinations are perceptual disorders in which mental images arise without real objects, which, however, does not exclude the possibility of an involuntary, indirect reflection of a person's previous life experience in hallucinations.

I was able to form a working therapeutic alliance with the client, and she visited my office two to three times a week. Most of the sessions were conducted in a dialogic manner, in which we interacted with each other, and occasionally the difficulties of her relationship with her parents were mentioned. For a long time my client preferred to ignore the problems of her hallucinatory symptoms and the fact that she was cut off from society; she could simply literally keep silent for an hour without saying a word after my cautious question on the subject.

But at one session, she took the initiative to talk about her social isolation and talked about her fear of other young people. Further conversation and a small experiment led to the client's recalling the physical abuse she had experienced as a child from other children, her resentment, pain and current fear that it would definitely happen again, although years had passed since the event and no more violence had occurred in her life. This was a clear example of the projection of the negative past into the present and possible future, which caused her fear of social contacts, and as a result, we managed to work productively with this material. After many sessions of just talking, it was finally possible to do what seemed to be progressive psychotherapeutic work, and I was very pleased with this result by the end of the session.

How unexpected it was for me when the next day I received a call from the client's parents telling me that the girl refused to come to my sessions anymore, believing that her mother and father were in cahoots with me and that the purpose of this conspiracy was to bring her to the grave. She described me as a "sadist who pretends to be trying to help her, but enjoys her pain and suffering and wants to bring her to the grave" by causing mental anguish. Her parents tried to convince her that this was not he case, but this only served to reinforce the girl's delusion that we were all villains who wanted to harm her, since her father and mother trusted me and the work I did.

In a short period of time, the client formed a power-ful delusion that included me and her parents. There was no rational explanation for this situation. It was impossible to convince the client because of the uncritical nature of the delusion. I asked her parents to tell my client that her sessions hours were up to her, and I would wait for her to return. I hoped that the productive psychotherapeutic alliance formed in the past would bring her back to my office.

But my client simply skipped some sessions, came to others, but remained silent throughout the sessions, keeping her heavy gaze on me. All my attempts to establish contact with her were unsuccessful.

The therapeutic breakthrough in this situation was facilitated by supervision, which I occasionally took from my colleague who specialized in working with people with psychotic disorders. The material that I received as a result of the supervisory analysis literally turned my professional consciousness upside down and opened up new insights into working with delusional clients. Since this book is intended to be educational, I will briefly leave the description of my client's case and present some theoretical and methodological aspects of this issue.

An important feature of clients with psychotic conditions is that they require much more emotional openness from the Gestalt therapist in communication than other clients who come to us with other problems. With people suffering from neuroses, the psychotherapist discloses himself in a controlled manner only within the framework of the client's request and he or she does it in order, for example, to awaken feelings, strengthen and raise the Id-function in the other participant in the session. But a client with a psychotic disorder does not need this, they need the behavior and emotions of the Gestalt therapist to be clearly understood by them. If this understanding is not there, then these clients will begin to look for answers in their projective fantasies about the psychotherapist's emotional manifestations that they do not understand (McWilliams, 1994).

When a psychotic client engages in distorted projection, it does not mean that their projection is aimed at disrupting the establishment of contact or actively contradicting the conditions of reality. Projection, like other coping mechanisms, is initially a normal way of adjustment and is an intuitive sensory attempt by the psychotic client to understand another human being and to be in authentic interaction with him or her in the context of a conscious environment, which in its effort brings him or her closer to the therapist and other people who do not suffer from delusions. When a client in a psychotic state includes the attitude of his Gestalt therapist in the delusional plot and grotesquely misinterprets therapist's behavior, they are simply looking for an answer about the feelings of another person that are incomprehensible or disturbing to them and may go too far in their search. It is important for a psychotherapist to keep this in mind when interacting with such a client - the feelings you demonstrate must be explained sincerely and simply.

It is also important for the psychotherapist to remember that there is always some truth in the most paranoid client's constructs (McWilliams, 1994). In psychotherapy, it is extremely important to direct research towards finding the rational grain of delusions, since the psychotic projection carried out by a person can catch a shade of truth about the feelings of the Gestalt therapist, but due to the lack of therapeutic involvement and transparency, it can end up being too distorted, sometimes to an absurd extent.

And now, after some theoretical pause, let us return to my client's case. In the course of supervision, I consistently reviewed the details of the last session with the client, after which she developed the delusion that "*I enjoy her suffering and only want bad things for her*". It was the supervisor's focus on what was true in her interpretation of my reactions that provided a rational interpretation of the delusion and the situation.

As I mentioned earlier in the text, I was pleased that the client and I were able to get to the traumatic situation from childhood and work productively with it, and this was quite different from the previous talking sessions, it seemed to be a progressive moment in the problem of social isolation. I was happy with the result - I felt satisfied. I didn't jump for joy, I didn't clap my hands, I didn't smile, but I was satisfied with the session and this satisfaction somehow was reflected on my face.

My client, for the first time after many sessions in which we hadn't discussed the problems that hindered her adjustment, agreed and touched on the difficult issue of her isolation, which then plunged her into the painful topic of childhood physical abuse. And when she was able to experience the intense pain, and by the end of the session she realized that she was probably avoiding and afraid of other young people because of the memory of her past trauma, but that this traumatic event did not have to happen again, she recognized a reaction of pleasure in me. She did not understand this reaction, and I did not explain it. The combination of immersing the client in a painful topic and my unexplained pleasure reaction gave rise to delusions that I was enjoying her suffering and wishing her the worst, namely death.

Of course, my awareness of the situation between us was a working supervisory hypothesis that needed to be tested. At the next session, when the client was sitting on the couch, looking at me again with a tense, distrustful look and remaining silent, I very carefully started a conversation about the previous session, after which her delusional negative attitude became the figure of our contact.

I carefully shared my hypothesis, tried to explain how I felt at that moment, what was really the reason for my satisfaction with the work. I said that no psychotherapy can avoid tears and severe pain, and that sometimes in order to build a happy present, you have to touch the emotional wounds of the past and cleanse them of suffering.

I explained to the client, using a metaphor I had heard once, that such a psychotherapeutic action is similar to opening an abscess - it almost always causes pain and is sometimes the only necessary condition. I was as sincere as possible in my self-disclosure. The client listened to me in silence and, as always, left the room silently at the end of the session.

But the next time she started talking at the session. Little by little, she opened up about what was bothering her. At the end of the week, she apologized to me for her behavior, for thinking badly of me, and said she wanted to give me a gift. I said in response that the newfound trust between us was already a great gift for me. The delusion symptoms dissolved. And we moved on to work on her problems. Further psychotherapy lasted for about a year, and the client eventually entered a stable remission.

I am very grateful for the lesson I learned when this psychotic projection was put on me. Since then, I have been very attentive to what I feel, reveal, or hold onto in my work with such clients, always explaining my emotional reactions to them and remembering the kernel of truth that can live in even the most fanciful structure of thought disorders.

At the end of this chapter, which is devoted to the issues of accompanying clients who organize their delusion through the projection of the idea of, I think it is also important to emphasize the opinion of Ginger & Ginger (1987) and his psychoanalytic colleague Racamier (1967) that psychotherapeutic behavior in working with psychotic suffering at the highest level of work is similar to parental support. After all, a good father protects.

A psychotherapist, like a parent, protects the client from the outside world and protects the client from himself or herself - all those powerful and destructive impulses and distortions that are tearing outward. This is how he or she takes care of the suffering human soul.

REFERENCES

1. Ginger S., Ginger A. (1987). *La Gestalt, une thérapie du contact*. Hommes et Groupes, Paris.
2. McWilliams N. (1994). *Psychoanalytic diagnosis: Understanding personality structure in the clinical process*. New York: The Guilford Press.
3. Perls F. (1947). *Ego, Hunger and Aggression: A Revision of Freud's Theory and Method*. The Gestalt Journal Press, Inc., Gouldsboro.
4. Perls F. (1973). *The Gestalt Approach & Eye Witness to Therapy*. New York. Bantam Books.
5. Polster E., Polster M. (1973). *Gestalt Therapy Integrated: Contours of Theory and Practice*. Brunner-Mazel, New York.
6. Racamier P. (1967). *Psychotherapie psychanalytique des psychose. - La psychanalyse d'aujourd'hui* (édité par S. Nacht.) Paris, PUF.

CHAPTER 3

GESTALT THERAPY
IN THE WORLD OF
HISTRIONIC SUFFERING

RELEVANCE OF THE ISSUE

Patients suffering from conversion disorders can be found in different parts of a general somatic hospital - in the offices of neurologists, gastroenterologists, cardiologists, and sometimes ophthalmologists and laryngologists, where the symptoms of their disorder and the oppositional belief in the presence of an organic disease sometimes create diagnostic and therapeutic problems. People with the same syndromes who are treated in neurosis departments at psychiatric hospitals also keep their psychotherapists busy, who follow the legendary paths of Freud, Charcot, and Janet and try to unravel the mystery of their illness and then turn it into a simple human misfortune that can be mourned, experienced, and comprehended. In the private practice of psychological counseling, Gestalt therapists, like medical professionals, accompany their histrionic clients to help them explore the difficulties of their over-excited existence and the horizons moving toward which can help them transcend their conservative neurotic adjustment.

VARIETY OF SYMPTOMS AND DIAGNOSES

In classical psychiatry, hysteria or hysterical neurosis was understood as a disease caused by the effects of mental trauma, in the course of which the mechanism of "escape into illness" and "conditional pleasantness or desirability" of a painful symptom plays a role. The very concept of "conditional pleasantness or desirability" of a painful symptom suggests that simultaneously with the idea of the pleasantness of this symptom, a person has an idea of the opposite nature (Tölle, 1971). At present, the solution of diagnostic problems of hysterical disorders is complicated by the presence of numerous discrepancies in clinical terminology. For example, the term "hysteria" was not used in any of the titles of the Class V (F) ICD-10 headings because of the number and variety of its meanings. Instead, preference was given to the term "dissociative", which united disorders that were previously considered hysterical, both of dissociative and conversion types. This is largely due to the fact that patients with dissociative and conversion types of disorders often show a number of other common characteristics, and they often have manifestations of both types of symptoms at the same time or at different times. Experts justifiably believe that dissociative and conversion symptoms have the same (or very similar) psychological mechanisms of development.

Discrepancies among clinicians regarding the accepted classification schemes and definitions of histrionic issues is explained not only by the difference in their views on the very nature and determination of this disorder, but also by the wide heterogeneity of theories of neurosis and personality disorders, which differ depending on the authors' commitment to psychodynamic, cognitive, or humanistic-existential approaches.

Let's reveal the meaning of the concepts of "conversion" and "dissociation", which are currently used in modern psychiatry to denote the phenomena of what used to be called hysterical disorder. Conversion is the transformation of a repressed mental conflict into somatic symptoms. Conversion symptoms, reflecting the conflict symbolically, are aimed at benefitting from the disease (Tölle, 1971). For example, according to the "grandfather of Gestalt Therapy", Hungarian psychoanalyst Sandor Ferenczi, conversion paresis of the hand can be interpreted in a negative way as an intention to act aggressively, conversion cramp as a struggle of conflicting emotions, local anesthesia or hyperesthesia as a consciously fixed memory of sexual touching of the body (Ferenczi, 1950). Dissociation is a process that is difficult to describe: what is united is disintegrated here; combined mental processes are torn into some parts; something falls out of a full life and is not realized. This psychodynamic model is similar to this model of conversion reactions. However, the dissociation is manifested not by somatic symptoms, but by impaired mental functions, especially memory and self-esteem (Lingiardi & McWilliams, 2017; Tölle, 1971).

In order to avoid confusion in the wide variety of hysterical disorders and their definitions, throughout this book I will use the terms "dissociative conversion disorder" to refer to the symptomatic neurotic neoplasm and "histrionic personality" whenever I discuss personality structure and character pathology. Since my clients with these disorders were mostly young girls, I will tend to write about the issues of "histrionic personality" in the feminine gender. At the same time, I would like to note that modern clinical data and experience of psychotherapeutic practice of specialists in various fields confirm that histrionic problems are also observed in men, but are not so common (Кришталь,

Кришталь, Кришталь, 2008; McWilliams, 1994; Lingiardi & McWilliams, 2017).

The large and varied dissociative conversion symptoms can be divided into several blocks:

1. Sensory-motor disorders: various pathological bodily sensations that mimic topographically limited sensory disorders (skin anesthesia or hyperesthesia, partial or complete loss of hearing, vision, or smell), often associated with motor or coordination disorders (paralysis, astasia[14] - abasia[15] phenolmena). It is worth noting that these disorders of the sensory-motor sphere in modern psychiatry are classified as conversion disorders.

2. Vegetosomatic disorders: vomiting, constipation, flatulence, nausea, tachycardia. They can mimic various patterns observed in the clinic of internal medicine. Sometimes disorders of autonomic functions present significant diagnostic difficulties, especially if they are superimposed on certain nonconversion disorders of internal organs, causing exacerbations and relapses of the disease. In the clinical picture of conversion disorder with body fantasies, along with elementary and unstable painful sensations, more complex ones are observed: the feeling of a "balloon inflating in the stomach", a lump in the throat (globus hystericus), perceived as a voluminous bodily neoplasm.

---

[14] Astasia is the loss of the ability to stand without the support of another person. It is observed in organic lesions of the central nervous system and in dissociative conversion disorder.

[15] Abasia is the loss of the ability to stand and walk, although in a lying position a person shows the ability to perform movements with sufficient strength and volume. It is often combined with astasia. It is characteristic of dissociative conversion disorder.

3. Emotional disorders: emotional lability, impulsivity, deliberately demonstrative nature of complaints.

4. Mental disorders: short-term hallucinations with a bright emotional coloring and theatrical and dramatic nature of experiences, dissociative fugue[16], pseudodementia[17], dissociative amnesia[18]. In these disorders, the leading process is dissociation.

5. Sexual disorders: anorgasmia[19], alibidemia[20], hyperactualization or disactualization of sexual function.

It is a well-known fact in psychiatry that the picture of conversion disorders varies from era to era and differs from country to country. The frequent, vivid, detailed attacks in the form of "posessions" that were common in the Middle Ages have now disappeared, psychotic mental disorders have become less common, and vegetosomatic and sensorimotor disorders in the form of hypochondriacal manifestations have begun to dominate the picture of disorders. Modern phobias began to show a lot of "histrionics" with the characteristic tinge of deliberate and exaggerated visual demonstration of fear and the theatricalized colorfulness of its experiences.

---

[16] Dissociative fugue is a disorder that occurs due to psychological trauma in histrionic individuals, in which a person not only forgets the past, but can also go to an unfamiliar place and imagine themselves as another person.

[17] Pseudodementia is one of the variants of dissociative reactions in histrionic personalities, characterized by symptoms of inarticulateness, mimicry, and a picture of an imaginary decrease in the level of intellectual activity.

[18.] Dissociative amnesia is the inability to recall important events or information related to one's personal life, usually of an unpleasant nature.

[19.] Anorgasmia is the absence of orgasm during sexual intercourse.

[20.] Alibidemia is the absence of sexual desire

Due to the increased suggestibility and autosuggestibility of people with conversion disorders, their prolonged stay in a somatic or neurological hospital, together with severe somatic patients, can be a source of additional somatovegetative and pseudo-motor disorders. I have repeatedly observed this phenomenon in the department of gastroenterology, where I worked for several years, when patients with a histrionic personality structure who were treated for a conversion disorder, initially accepted by doctors as, say, functional dyspepsia, began to present, over time, various gastroenterological and somatovegetative symptoms, and sometimes motor disorders observed in other patients from the neighboring neurology department.

A further detailed examination of all possible symptoms of conversion and dissociative disorders seems rather cumbersome and goes beyond this manuscript, as it requires the writing of an entire clinical monograph on this issue. Below, we will consider some rather specific syndromes of histrionic suffering in the context of their translation into the language of Gestalt Therapy and possible psychotherapeutic strategies for working with them.

A histrionic personality is characterized by egocentrism, increased suggestibility, theatricality, seductiveness, and exaggerated expression of emotions, a tendency to cry, easy vulnerability, predominance of affects over reason, excessive preoccupation with theit attractiveness, and constant preferences (McWilliams, 1994; Lingiardi & McWilliams, 2017). Histrionic personality disorder[21], like other variants of character pathology, manifests itself clearly in adolescence, tends to be ego-syntonic and is characterized by periods of severe social disadaptation.

_____

[21] A personality disorder is a personality anomaly characterized by persistent mental disharmony and formed mainly in adolescence.

THE CONTRIBUTION OF PSYCHOANALYSIS AND EXISTENTIALISM TO GESTALT THERAPY OF HISTRIONIC PROBLEMS

Modern experts in Gestalt Therapy recognize that some concepts of the psychoanalytic paradigm, such as transference-countertransference[22], regression, and the level of personality organization, can be useful and valuable for promoting Gestalt Therapy, especially in cases where clients have severe psychopathological problems of the psychotic or borderline spectrum (Ginger & Ginger, 1987). In this regard, the understanding of histrionic suffering by the classics of psychodynamic psychotherapy is of interest to our study. I would like to note that in the time of Freud, Jung, Boss, and other fundamental authors, dissociative conversion disorder and histrionic personality disorder were defined as "hysteria" and therefore, when referring to them, I will use this term, authentic to their scientific works.

Thus, in 1895, Freud and his teacher Breyer came to the conclusion that the main factor in the origin of hysteria is psychological trauma, if it is understood in the sense of a negative mental experience (any event associated with the experience of fear, shame, guilt). However, in Freud's final theory, the emphasis was shifted to the fact that hysteria is based on both the factor of Oedipus's sexual complex and the factor of displaced psychotraumas of early childhood development with a sexual context (Jakubik, 1979; Lingiardi & McWilliams, 2017).

---

[22] Countertransference is a set of conscious and especially unconscious processes of the psychotherapist caused by the client's personality (and, in particular, his or her transfer). Countertransference is everything that is caused by the therapist's personality and can affect their relationship with the client (Ginger, 1995).

The founder of analytical psychology, Carl Jung, believed that hysteria is an extreme form of extraversion, which is manifested by extreme orientation towards the outside world and disregard for introverted attitudes, leading to the threat of losing one's Self [23,] projection of one's own negative properties onto others, and disruption of the compensation of the conscious and unconscious, which should contribute to the mental balance of the personality. Hysteria is an inhibition in the process of individuation, which, according to Jung, normally includes two phases: in the first half of life, a person's task is to adapt to external reality, and in the second half - to internal reality. Hysteria is a kind of prolonged first phase, characterized not only by the one-sided predominance of the extroverted attitude, but also by the underdevelopment and undifferentiation of all four functions of the psyche, which is manifested mainly by a low degree of awareness and stability of the Self. Hysterical somatic and mental symptoms seem to force a person to take into account the introverted attitudes that have been displaced by them (Jakubik, 1979).

The author of interpersonal psychoanalysis, Harry Stack Sullivan, mainly dealt with schizophrenia, but histrionic issues also attracted his attention. For example, he described hysterical neurosis as a peculiar form of interpersonal relationships, and even considered them in the categories of a special type of behavior - a game, the purpose of which is to achieve the approval of others, thus ensuring a sense of security (Jakubik, 1979).

It is worth noting that Gestalt Therapy equally recognizes the possibility of the existence of the above-described views of the psychoanalysis classics on understanding the essence of hysteria, but rather for individual, concrete and specific cases of histrionic suffering, and not using these concepts as a universal theoretical application to all cases of clinical practice.

---

[23] Here "Self" is used not in reference to a process, but to an entity.

But now let's talk about the contribution of modern psychoanalysis to Gestalt Therapy. Among the psychoanalytic concepts close to our approach, which explain the origin of mental disorders primarily as a violation of external relations with the environment, rather than as a consequence of repressed impulses emanating from basic instincts, a special place is taken by the theories of object relations reflected in the works by Winnicott, Balint, and other psychoanalysts. According to the founders of this approach, motivation is based on the fundamental human need for relationships, and the structure of the personality is formed in the process of internalizing relationships, while the problems of individual development are not related to the stages of psychosexual development, but to the variability of the human being's struggle for belonging, and, at the same time, for separation from his or her family. Modern Gestalt Therapy integrates theoretical and methodological developments of this psychoanalysis branch, thus enriching clinical practice and methodology. For example, the director of NeuroGestalt, a specialist group in the International Neuro-psychoanalysis Society, a French psychotherapist Delisle (1991) devoted his scientific thesis to this topic and in his practice and publications on the specifics of Gestalt Therapy in the treatment of personality disorders, he clearly and perfectly demonstrated the complementarity of approaches, considering the development of a pathological personality as a phenomenon of the field - the field as it was understood by Gestalt psychologist Kurt Lewin. The author argues that the structure of the psyche is formed in the process of internalizing relationships with significant objects.

Summarizing the data of the famous American psychoanalyst McWilliams (1994), and translating them into the language of Gestalt Therapy, it can be noted that object relations in histrionic individuals are characterized by the fact that a person learns to adapt initially in such an environment (family system) where there are regulations on granting men more power than women. Often, in such families, a special "masculine" strength is cultivated, but faults and possible personal shortcomings are seen as manifestation of "femininity". In such families, the father often has a narcissistic personality structure, he loves and frightens his child, is distant from caring for his daughter, and this makes him more attractive for idealization and endowing him with a fan of projections, forming him into a figure of the Mighty Other. As a result of such upbringing, a woman devalues her own feminine traits, deprives herself of female self-respect, and her personality throughout her life is characterized by a sense of being a small, fearful, and defective child, since positive reinforcement in her family extended only to her infantile traits, good looks, and frivolous attributes in behavior. All she takes from femininity is sexuality, because for her it is the only thing in a woman that has a strange, sometimes magical power over men.

In seeking relationships colored by her affection for strong men, she uses her sexuality and often fails in her personal and intimate life. In fact, it is not so much the need for sexual contact that is relevant for her, but rather the need for self-respect and a sense of security, for which sexualization of relationships is only a common and often the only means. In other words, we can consider such eroticization as a manifestation of deflection[24], as a workaround, as manipulation that can be realized to a different extent or not be realized at all. A direct contact with the environment - that part of the psychological field that significantly affects human behavior - threatens a histrionic personality with strong emotional tension and is therefore partially replaced in their life space by "virtual contact".

---

[24] Deflection is a resistance that is used to change either the object or the actions in relation to this object. A person resists deflection in order to avoid the emotional stress of direct contact.

It is as if the woman meets again and again with the figures and relationships of the family in which she grew up, with its rules and norms, and obeys them in the mode of conservative adjustment.

In this process, the traits of the other are projected onto the real male partner; manipulative eroticization destroys true intimacy between partners, depriving them of protection from the existential given called "loneliness", frustrating their needs for security and acceptance in relationships in the usual way.

Because of the "unimportant" relationship with their mother in the family system, histrionic women have virtually no female friends in their adult lives, as they often projectively experience the Other Adult Woman not only as an "evil rival" but also as a devalued "weak rag", which excludes the search for warmth and security in such relationships. And this makes the partner dyad with a man extremely tense due to its isolation. Histrionic women of the borderline level of personality organization usually choose straightforward, aggressive men with a strong sexual appeal (macho type) as their partners and expect these men to give them everything at once - the strength of a father and husband, as well as tenderness and pity (basic security), which is usually more characteristic for a mother's position. Even if their aggressive partners are capable of giving these things, they turn out to be "bad" in each of their manifestation, being insufficient. The vicious circle closes, and this adds another weighty brick to the foundation of histrionic unhappiness.

It is now time to discuss the contribution of existential philosophy and psychotherapy to the Gestalt Therapy of histrionic suffering. According to Ginger & Ginger (1987), the Gestalt approach borrows the following important general concepts from existentialism:

1. Concrete experience is more important than abstract principles.

2. The originality of each human existence, the originality of individual human experience, both objective and subjective.

3. The concept of responsibility is inherent in everyone who takes an active part in the implementation of their own existential project and gives a special, original meaning to what happens to them and the world around them, tirelessly creating their relative freedom every day.

An original and, in my opinion, close to Gestalt Therapy view of understanding histrionic suffering is presented in the existential-phenomenological psychotherapy of Medard Boss. The author believed that hysteria is equal to a person's refusal of freedom and "openness to the world", thus it is equal to the need to transfer all relations with the world to a "wordless" sphere of existence - to the sphere of corporeality, since the latter is an intermediary between the "I" and the environment. Transferring interpersonal relations that have never been there into the sphere of bodily relations with the world causes the boundaries of the bodily to be "inflated" and indicates pathological disorders in this sphere of human existence. Because of this, the image of "being-in-the-world" becomes one-sided and limited to communication with the world in the form of wordless communication. As an example, such a symptom as hysterical writing convulsion, according to Boss, symbolically expresses the "compression" of the hitherto "open" human world and is the opposite of freedom, that is, it is coercion, restriction (Jakubik, 1979).

In his publication, Ginger (1995) argues that for histrionic individuals, the temptation or seduction of the environment is overcautiousness against basic existential anxiety, and only after that it is possible to adapt and connect with this part of the psychological field.

SPECIFICS OF GESTALT THERAPY
FOR CLIENTS WITH HISTRIONIC SUFFERING

The director of the Institute of Gestalt Therapy in Nantes, Blaize (2001), connects histrionic issues with the radical existential insufficiency of a person's holistic access to their organic body, i. e. with the inability to see themselves as one can see any other human being. The author argues that some body parts, such as the back of the head or a part of the back, are completely inaccessible to the human gaze, and technical devices (mirror, camera, video) change the very structure of the body image. The histrionic problematics is a search for ways to replenish this insufficiency, to gain confidence, but in this case - by attracting the attention of another person, so that this other person could return to me the part of me that I own and that is always eluding me.

American Gestalt therapists from the Gestalt Institute of Cleveland, Melnick & Nevis (1992), speaking about histrionic personality disorder, emphasize that people with this type of disorders are characterized by the impossibility of an existential phenomenological encounter with the Other; they can see, speak, laugh, hug with an excess of excitement, but they very often do not feel deeply interested in the other participant, in the fact that he or she is also there, that is, he or she also listens, sees, speaks, and such such a hug can be overly passionate for him, be an inappropriate way of contact. The histrionic personality has "too much energy" in contact, but at the same time this contact is minimally filled, and the psychotherapist's attempt to establish it meets, according to the authors, indifference or opposition, which can be expressed, in my observations, sometimes in ridicule and devaluation, that is, the actualization of such resistances as deflection and invalidation[25].

---

[25] Invalidation is a resistance that blocks the appropriation of experience and changes in the worldview.

Quite apt and sad in its own way is the remark of Cleveland Gestalt therapists that such clients are almost not interested in awareness because it will make their lives more difficult and less exciting (Melnick & Nevis, 1992). In fact, this is indeed the case.

At the same time, very often such a client can learn the terms of the Gestalt approach from their psychotherapist, repeat them, assure their psychotherapist of "the breadth of their awareness, the closure of the gestalts", but in fact we face a client's refusal to be aware of their behavioral patterns and to seek changes in their way of being.

In the context of this topic, I would like to give an example from my practice of psychotherapeutic work with a teenage girls who had a distinct histrionic radical and committed pseudo-suicide in a general somatic hospital - she cut her arms after finding out that her new boyfriend had decided to break up with her. In the course of psychotherapy, which lasted several sessions, this patient often asked me for direct advice on what she should do next with her boyfriend, how she could get him back and control him. At the same time, she refused in every possible way from any experiments aimed at expanding her understanding of herself and the situation she was organizing, often going into empty conversations, supported by an abundant flow of tears. The fragment below is an excerpt from the last session with her before she was discharged from the hospital:

> C: Yevgeny Mykolayovych, I want to thank you for these sessions that I have had with you, and especially for today's one, I have understood so much, a lot, you have opened my eyes to the world, I understand so much now, I have learned so many life lessons!
> T: Thank you. But I have a question for you... Tell me exactly what you understood in our sessions, give me a couple of

examples of what you have learned. (Silence follows. There is confusion on the girl's face, which is changed to anger).
C: Why are you doing this to me, Yevgeny Mykolayovych? I tell you that you are a good man, and you ask me these strange questions!
T: Do you notice what happens to you after I ask you a question? Take your time, please pay attention to how you are behaving now.
C: There is nothing to pay attention to - I'm just angry with you! What strange people you, psychologists, are! You tell them "good things, thank you", and they seem to mock you with their stupid questions!

The phenomena of the diversity of pathological disorders and lack of interest in awareness in the histrionic personality lead me to the hypothesis that in clients with this psychopathology, there is a global problem of the possibility of the holistic coexistence of these two processes. Thus, in the theoretical postulates of Gestalt Therapy, there is an opinion about the close relationship between arousal as a source of energy and awareness, since the former provides physiological reinforcement to the latter, is embodied and manifested in feelings and sensory sensations, and the latter forms a powerful and stable experience of personality's integrity (Polster, 1995). In a person with histrionic issues, there is a distortion of this organismic relationship with a great predominance and hypertrophy of the arousal process, and hence the impossibility of building a clear, complete and balanced contact with the social environment.

Based on the fact that a histrionic personality is not interested in the depth of relationships with environmental figures, the strategic task of a Gestalt therapist in working with this category of clients is to accompany them to the polar position of relations with the world - building new complex contacts with others, awakening interest in dialogue. According to Melnik & Nevis (1992), to achieve this task, experiments on teaching such people to notice environmental contexts (situations, relationships), taking into account other people, bring good results. It is also useful for the client to ask questions to the psychotherapist, as well as to notice and say out aloud the physical and physiological limitations that exist for them.

Another useful focus of the Gestalt therapist's work in the psychotherapy of histrionic personalities is to help the client slow down their own excessive rate of pathological arousal and provide an opportunity to withdraw into themselves, into their inner world, for better understanding, awareness of their needs, desires, and motives before taking action. If we translate psychoanalytic and Gestalt terminology, then in fact, this focus of work pays much attention to the development of such an analytical defense as acting out, which is very typical for histrionic personalities (McWilliams, 1994). This defense is an impulsive way of spilling out one's feelings and impulses with the inability to hold on to them, to focus on them. In Gestalt Therapy, this defense can be defined as a sign of a deficit of healthy retroreflection, and it will be strategically important for the psychotherapist to teach his or her client to master this way of contact. In order to achieve this, it is necessary to teach a person to concentrate on their own breathing, posture, gestures, movements, muscle tension, and voice timbre and slow them down, i.e. to transfer them from the mode of conservative adjustment to the mode of creative adjustment, and then observe how this changes the client and their relationship with the environment.

In my opinion, a rather interesting strategic step in Gestalt Therapy of histrionic issues may also be the testing of the proposal of Serge Ginger, the founder of the Paris School of Gestalt, to use the "polarities"[26] concept in order to balance different personality tendencies or expand the rigid personality radical.

The author proposes to encourage a histrionic personality in the course of psychotherapy to acquire features of the polar obsessive configuration, to develop behavioral "obsessions" (daily routine, programming, organization) that can be tested in the safe environment of individual or group psychotherapy (1995).

Working with histrionic suffering requires a certain amount of vigilance and judgment on the part of the psychotherapist, as they can easily get carried away by histrionic expression with its inherent emotionality and make a hasty mistake, in particular, engage in symptomatic treatment, to which clients can sometimes respond with a rapid reduction in symptoms. However, there is a risk in the latter case, since, according to Ginger (1995), certain histrionic manifestations, such as the pleasure of being seen or the desire to seduce others, can maintain the welcomed and necessary narcissism and thus avoid the establishment of permanent and pathological arousal.

It is also worth noting that there are differences in the attitudes toward psychotherapy among clients with histrionic suffering, depending on whether it is in the form of inpatient treatment in a general somatic hospital or neurosis department or in the form of private psychological practice. In an inpatient hospital environment, these patients are much less likely to be focused on solving their problems related to conversion symptomatology and pathological personality traits and are more likely to show the notorious "escape into illness" and "conditional pleasantness or desirability of the existing disorder".

[26.] Polarities – Gestalt Therapy strives for the harmonious unity of all complementary extremes (polarities) of human behavior (e. g., aggressiveness and tenderness), but without abandoning one extreme in favor of the other or without the illusory search for a "false" middle ground – a pale semblance of living feelings (Ginger, 1995).

When they seek psychological help on their own in private paid consultations outside the hospital, they are more likely to be motivated by a genuine desire to understand themselves and what they do to themselves and others, and how they organize their suffering.

As I have already mentioned, in the contemporary practice of psychiatry and psychotherapy we have to observe many different combinations of histrionic problems and it is impossible to describe all strategies of work with them from the standpoint of Gestalt Therapy within the framework of this manuscript. However, before concluding, I would like to give an example of Gestalt understanding of two rather specific histrionic sufferings, which include problems of memory and self-awareness.

PROBLEMS OF DISSOCIATIVE MEMORY

At the outset, I would like to note that diagnosed cases of dissociative amnesia are quite rare in psychiatric and psychotherapeutic practice, although this syndrome is described in detail in ICD-10, psychiatric monographs and textbooks, and in the classical psychoanalytic literature it takes the place of an important exhibit (Ferenczi, 1950; Jakubik, 1979; Lingiardi & McWilliams, 2017; Tölle, 1971). At the same time, in clinical practice, my colleagues and I have to observe phenomena characterized by the fact that clients suffering from dissociative-conversion disorders have significant difficulties when it comes to recalling certain episodes from their personal lives. For example, they may forget important events related to interpersonal separation, family conflicts, experiences of emotional intimacy, freedom, sexuality, loneliness, and sometimes they "do not remember" even entire milestones of their existence, which are calculated in months and years. In most cases, the phenomena of incomplete memories of events are recorded, and, as a rule, in the course of psychotherapy, this reveals the patient's desire to hide memories of mental trauma in the deep and dark basement of their inner reality and leave them there under seven seals. Dissociative amnesia and the described phenomena of "pseudo-forgetfulness" are based on the same mechanism of symptom development described in detail by psychoanalysts - displacement (aka repression). The histrionic personality undoubtedly knows how to skillfully delete his or her memory, sometimes cutting out large pieces of canvas from the picture of his or her life, capturing memories of joyful days along with painful memories.

Displacement is a defense characteristic of histrionic personalities and, according to psychoanalysts, is the removal of the memory of unpleasant experiences from the conscious to the unconscious level. As a rule, a histrionic personality takes this step because of a strong fear of deep emotional pain associated with memories of those events. From the standpoint of Gestalt Therapy, the displacement mechanism can be defined as *a nonspecific confluence 1 with one's own memories and the emotions associated with them.*

It seems important to make a couple of clarifications. First, the memory of events itself is not eliminated; rather, the connection with this memory is eliminated. In this case, the client can restore the gaps, but then he or she will have to take the risk of fully reliving the forgotten, blocked episodes of personal biography with all the corresponding emotional experiences and take responsibility for what happened (histrionic personalities often do not know how to share responsibility). Secondly, nonspecific confluence 1, although organizing these dissociative phenomena of psychopathology, does not cause the symptoms, but acts as a means of pathological avoidance of fear of pain and recognition of the fact of human misfortune.

Following the paradigm of Gestalt Therapy, it becomes obvious that blocking painful memories directly fixes the inability to complete the unfinished Gestalt. In order for the work on completing the unfinished drama (which requires efforts to react and comprehend what happened) to be done, it is necessary to return the forgotten pieces of memory, at least if the client has such a desire. This can be motivated by the hope, conveyed by the psychotherapist, that this will help reduce dissociative-conversion symptoms and return all the forgotten fragments to their rightful owner in order to put the mosaic together and build the present and future in a new way.

In experimental work with this type of nonspecific confluence, it will be useful to suggest that the client relax, focus on his or her even breathing, and then imagine his or her life or its separate segments in the form of a photo album, depending on the strategic and tactical goals of the session and the specifics of amnestic suffering, and then try to review them. Those years, months or important events that are not available to the client's visualization are "blind spots", a blockade from painful memories and unclosed gestalts, and the choice of further strategic work is directed towards them.

The nuances of further procedural work with the confluence 1 are usually well known to Gestalt therapists: it is the collecting a mosaic from separate fragments, an attempt to assemble a complete figure from individual phenomenological signs that are alienated from the client's awareness (posture, voice, movements, microgestures) using experimental techniques of "mirroring", amplification[27], and directed awareness.

[27.] Amplification is a classic experimental technique in Gestalt Therapy. It is an encouragement for the client to amplify their automatic gestures, sensations, or spontaneous feelings. This allows the client to become more aware of them through greater expressiveness. (Ginger, 1995)

Since the way out of the confluence 1 is fraught with the client's facing his or her own emotional pain on a large scale, an important task for the psychotherapist will be to create an atmosphere of warmth and trust in the therapist-client field, to provide support for these experiences through his or her own look, touch, and creating physical comfort for the client (taking a comfortable position, covering the client with a blanket or rug). Psychotherapeutic behavior in the context of this situation is more "maternal", but the position of a healthy paternal influence can also be extremely valuable - it may be important for a woman-client with histrionic issues to feel that she is under the protection of a "father" who is ready to provide her with safety in times of fear and pain, to accept her as she is, and not to reject her "weaknesses" - femininity, vulnerability, and the ability to sensually demonstrate her pain.

This new actual experience of healthy parental behavior on the part of the therapist may be an unknown facet that the client has never known in her life, as her own narcissistic father demanded that she be masculine and devalued her femininity. In this new contact for the client, a discovery takes place: *"you can be yourself, you can be loved and supported, and you don't need to seduce others, try to take a strong masculine position, you don't need to disguise yourself"*.

> As an example, I would like to tell the case of a young 17-year-old girl who, during her long-term psychotherapy, decided to engage in self-exploration by participating in an experiment in which she had to visualize a photo album of her life. She had previously mentioned her forgetfulness, which she failed to "compensate for with an organizer". During the experiment, she could not see the "photo" of the fourteenth year of her life with her inner look, while she remembered everything else well. Working with this year's blockage very quickly brought the client to a

situation of emotional alienation from her past, when she was abandoned by her father, who left for "another family". At first, the girl tried her best to get her father back, but after unsuccessful attempts, she began to deliberately dress informally and bizarrely, wearing eccentric make-up and hairstyles, and going out with a new group of "hippie" friends in places in the city where her father's high-ranking friends used to go. She wanted these friends to tell her father what they had seen and make him feel ashamed of his daughter. This "revenge" was supposed to ensure contact with her father, in which he would scold her for this behavior, but still be close to her, at least a little bit. But nothing happened according to the girl's plan - it resulted in her father's even colder detachment from her. Working on the response, completing the gestalt in an atmosphere of trust and support, understanding her place in the family drama that had unfolded, not only helped to heal the old emotional wound, but brought something else important - the client recalled all the joyful and significant events from that year of her life that were important to her, but remained hidden for so long behind the veil of forgetfulness of memory due to a strong traumatic event.

HISTRIONIC
DEPERSONALIZATION-DEREALIZATION

In histrionic depersonalization, a person is not convinced of real changes in their own personality, as it happens in depressive depersonalization or in cases of alienation in paranoid schizophrenia, when the patient is convinced that changes in perception are caused by other people or magical forces. In contrast to endogenous diseases, depersonalizing experiences are relatively simple, not bizarre, and a person always treats them as unreal phenomena, that is, as something that only seems. Histrionic symptoms are expressed in the form of somatopsychic depersonalization (alienation of the body, some parts of it, feeling of alienation of one's voice, feeling of slowing down of one's own movements) and derealization (feeling of unreality of the environment, when it is perceived as if through a veil, film, objects look colorless, monochromatic, distorted, devoid of interest) (Jakubik, 1979).

In psychodynamic-oriented psychiatry, depersonalization syndrome is viewed through the prism of the action of the deep defense mechanisms of the "Ego" against an overwhelming emotional experience, in particular, an aggressive impulse towards another person (Tölle, 1971). According to psychoanalysts, when in a stable mental state, a person perceives this impulse with a sense of guilt, while in a state of depersonalization, this impulse is perceived by a person as something that does not belong to him or her, is not authentic. To get into this state, a histrionic personality can mobilize his or her characteristic defense - regression to an early childhood thinking and ways of experiencing that correspond to the age when the structure of the "Ego" and the attitude towards reality were not yet stable. The phenomenon of unconscious regressive transition to a less mature cognitive functioning that provides a sense of security in tense situations is, in the categories of Gestalt Therapy, a nonspecific confluence 1 with a person's own mature cognitive structures. It is worth noting that such a confluence usually lives alongside the projection of one's own cognitive capacities onto a status figure (father, husband) or onto a psychotherapist: *"Doctor, I am so little, helpless, I don't know what to do in this situation, and you are the most intelligent, wisest, tell me what to do"*.

As an example, here is another fragment from the psychotherapy of one of my clients. At one of the first sessions, she told me about her state of depersonalization-derealization, which had become an integral part of her daily life. During her story, she began to suddenly fall into this state right in my office.

C: (The client is lying on the couch, looking at the ceiling). Now I'm falling into this state... I'm becoming transparent...

T: How do you perceive the environment now?

C: I see myself as out of this world. In general, as if I were out of this world. The environment is becoming pleasant for me. (The girl's energy becomes low).

T: What happens to you when you feel like that?

C: It's like I'm not here. I mean, I am here, but people don't seem to notice me, and that makes me feel so good. (The voice and facial expressions are devoid of vitality, color.)

T: Do you still feel something like that?

C: Yes! And now you are sitting here, I am listening to you, perceiving you, but it is somehow dull, it is difficult to explain... I may not think about you, but I perceive you. What's happening to me is something that started about two months. It's like in the astral... It's so hard to explain... I feel like I'm disconnected from everything... I feel like I'm dissolving... Everything is distant, and the sounds and colors of these walls in the office... I don't hear anyone... It's very nice

T: I want you to try to slowly take the opposite body position now, look at me, look at the office, and notice what happens to you as you do so.

C: (The client does what I asked). There you go! I'm starting to think again.

T: How do you perceive me now?

C: Now I perceive you with character, now you are a personality, and there you were like on TV. Now you are more real, and there you were more distant.

T: Which people in your life would you like to distance? (I make a "mental shuttle[28]" from the "layer of being" of the therapeutic situation to the "layer" of relationships with environmental figures in the client's everyday life).

C: Oh! Dad... Mom, and something very general, like education... It's not education... Oh! It's a person! I would like to get rid of the teacher from the university who checks my thesis, I'm sick of her nagging me!

T: If you were to distance yourself from them, what would happen then? (I clarify which need is not being met and the symptoms are being organized).

C: Then it would be much better. I would really like to distance my father, because everything what is happening between us is complete rubbish. Rubbish from his side. I would like him not to be there.

T: Does your father know about these feelings you have? That you wish he wasn't there?

C: No. I can only talk about this in your office. It is possible to keep a secret here. It would be cool if my parents were not there. It would be cool if they were somewhere far away from me.

---

[28] The mental shuttle is an experimental technique of reverse "movement" between the external reality perceived in society and the internal reality, i.e. phenomenological or imaginary experience, between emotion and verbal awareness, between the client's everyday life and the metaphorical situation created here and now, during this psychotherapeutic session, as well as between the present and the past. This shuttle "movement" is widely used in Gestalt Therapy (Ginger, 1995).

T: How do you feel now that you've said that?
*C: It's important that I've said it. It's important for me
to talk about it. I could only tell my friend Oksana about it
before, but somehow I didn't dare to in the last few months,
and then I told you about it. It's hard to talk about such
things with other people when you want your family to be
away, because it makes you feel better.*

I will give a small commentary on the transcript used. In the above psychotherapy fragment, I explored the relationship between the psychopathological syndrome and the perception of the external environment in the course of the therapeutic situation, trying to clarify what happened to the client when this state was actualized and what happened when it was de-actualized, how the girl perceived me as an external figure in these two different modes of consciousness. This state of derealization-depersonalization is related to the functioning of the confluence 1, evidenced by the client's transition to low energy, vagueness and dullness of her sensory sensations. In this state, the client moved away from environmental figures, which probably helped her to protect herself from pain. After using the "mental shuttle" between different "layers of being", it became possible to find out that in everyday life the girl would like to distance herself from her mother, father and university teacher, as the relationship with them was full of tension, and their alienation implied a state of certain pseudo-stabilization.

REFERENCES
THE WORLD OF HISTRIONIC SUFFERING

1. Baalen van D. (2010). Gestalt Therapy and Bipolar Disorder. *Gestalt Review,* 14, 1: 71–88.
2. Blaize J. (2001). *Ne plus savoir. Phenomenologie et etique de la psychotherapie.* - Bordeaux: L'exprimerie, 2001.
3. Delisle G. (1991). A Gestalt Perspective of Personality Disorders. *British Gestalt Journal,* 1, 1: 42-50.
4. Ferenczi S. (1950). The phenomena of hysterical materialization, in.: *Contributions to the Theory and Technique of Psychoanalysis,* 2 Bde., L..
5. Ginger S., Ginger A. (1987). *La Gestalt, une thérapie du contact. Hommes et Groupes,* Paris.
6. Ginger S. (1995). *La Gestalt, l'art du contact.* Marabout, Paris.
7. Jakubik A. (1979). Histeria: Metodologia, teoria, psychopatologia. PZWL.
8. Lingiardi V., McWilliams N. (Eds.) (2017). *Psychodynamic Diagnostic Manual,* 2nd ed. New York: Guilford Press.
9. McWilliams N. (1994). *Psychoanalytic diagnosis: Understanding personality structure in the clinical process.* New York: The Guilford Press.
10. Melnick J. & Nevis S. M. (1992). Diagnosis: The Struggle for a Meaningful Paradigm, in Nevis E. C. (ed.), *Gestalt Therapy: Perspectives and Applications,* Gardner Press, New York.
11. Polster E. (1995). *A Population of Selves: A Therapeutic Exploration of Personal Diversity.* Gouldsboro, ME: The Gestalt Journal Press
12. Tölle R. (1971). *Psychiatrie einschließlich Psychotherapie.* Springer, Berlin Heidelberg.

AFTERWARD

There is a time to open gestalts and a time to close them...

This book has been written and completed, and now I hope it has been read by you, dear readers. I hope that it leaves a pleasant aftertaste and will be useful in your psychotherapy practice.

Of course, I am aware that the three types of mental suffering described in this book do not cover the entire vast area of psychopathology and that much remains unexplored. I hope that in the future I will return to the world of clinical Gestalt Therapy and write the next part, devoted to the understanding of psychological help for people suffering from phobias, hypochondria, and other various disorders.

Finally, I would like to say that clinical Gestalt Therapy does not aim to treat symptoms, but rather to experimentally search for ways to achieve changes that were previously inaccessible or avoided by a person, and instead of growth led to pathology. However, when we risk looking for these necessary keys to meta-changes together with a client, we almost always face great difficulties...

And the truth is that sometimes — in the process of psychotherapy — when we become aware of our life and review it and all the choices we have made in it, it is very difficult for us to find a place to experience joy, but we can find in these sessions the strength to do what we really need to do. For example, to let the past finally go. And to allow ourselves to be reborn in the present.

ABOUT THE AUTHOR

Yevgeny Ryaboy is the Head of the International Association for Experimental Gestalt Therapy (the organization was established in Ukraine in 2023).

He got a Master's degree on Psychology in Zaporizhzhia National University. He studied Gestalt Therapy with such teachers as Brigitte Martel Cayeux (France), Martin Masson (France), Dan Bloom (USA), Jay Levin (USA), Peter Schulthess (Switzerland), Nancy Amendt-Lyon (Austria), Peter Phillipson (United Kingdom) and many others.

In 2018, he completed an internship on post-traumatic stress disorder in the United States under the Open World International Program.

He has 16 years of psychological practice. During this time, he worked as a practical psychologist at the Zaporizhzhia Regional Clinical Children's Hospital and as a lecturer at the Department of Psychology at the Institute of Management and Law in Zaporizhzhia National Technical University (now Zaporizhzhia Polytechnic National University). For 10 years he has been working with the Kyiv Gestalt University as a trainer and accredited Gestalt therapist.

In 2015-2018, he participated in many projects implemented by UN funds in Zaporizhzhia and Donetsk regions. He worked with the population affected by the military conflict, was engaged in social and psychological adaptation of anti-terrorist operation veterans and the prevention of sexual violence among adolescents.

ABOUT THE AUTHOR

Together with his colleagues Olena Lysenko and Natalia Zlyhosteva, he initiated the creation of the Gestalt Therapy Division at the National Psychological Association of Ukraine at the end of 2023 and now heads it, engaging in moderating activities.

He has a valid membership in the following professional associations:

- The European Association for Gestalt Therapy.
- The Association for Humanistic Psychology.
- The National Psychological Association of Ukraine.

CLINICAL GESTALT THERAPY

BY YEVGENY RYABOY

───────────────────────

A REVIEW BY YARO STARAK

Title: *Exploring Wholeness: A Comprehensive Review of "Gestalt Therapy for Distress"*

Reading the book, I am aware that the author is focusing on a series of topics and so I decided to write this review with another "title" "Gestalt Therapy for Distress".

"Gestalt Therapy for Distress" offers a profound exploration of the application of Gestalt Therapy in helping clients navigate and alleviate distress. Written by YEVGENY RYABOY, the book provides a comprehensive and insightful guide for both therapists and individuals seeking a holistic approach to mental health.

One of the strengths of the book is its clear and accessible language, making complex Gestalt Therapy concepts understandable to a broad audience. The author blends theoretical foundations with practical examples, creating a well-rounded resource that is valuable for both beginners and experienced therapists.

The central theme revolves around the gestalt philosophy of wholeness and the integration of fragmented aspects of one's self. The book delves into how this approach can be particularly effective in addressing distress, as it encourages individuals to become more aware of their present experiences and take responsibility for their emotions.

The practical techniques and exercises outlined in the book are another highlight. The author introduces various gestalt interventions that can be easily adapted to different therapeutic settings. Case studies illustrate the application of these techniques, providing readers with real-world examples of how Gestalt Therapy can be transformative in addressing distress.

One notable aspect is the emphasis on the therapeutic relationship. The author underscores the importance of the therapist-client connection in Gestalt Therapy, promoting a collaborative and non-judgmental atmosphere that fosters self-exploration. This relational focus adds depth to the book and aligns with contemporary therapeutic approaches that recognize the significance of the therapeutic alliance.

Furthermore, the book addresses potential challenges and ethical considerations in Gestalt Therapy, offering a balanced perspective on its limitations. This acknowledgment of the approach's nuances adds credibility and pragmatism to the narrative.

In conclusion, "Gestalt Therapy for Distress" stands out as an exceptional resource in the field. It combines theoretical foundations, practical applications, and a compassionate approach to guide both therapists and clients toward a deeper understanding of distress and the path to healing. Whether you are a professional in the mental health field or an individual seeking self-help resources, this book is a valuable addition to your library.

Yaro Starak is an international teacher of Gestalt Therapy, co-director of the Gestalt Art Therapy Center (Australia), a founding member of Gestalt Australia & New Zealand (GANZ), an accreditation organization for of Gestalt Therapy training in Australia and New Zealand, author of the books *Risking Being Alive*, *Group Work Skills* and *The Princess and the Dragon*.

BIBLIOGRAPHY

1. Baalen van D. (2010). "Gestalt Therapy and Bipolar Disorder" *Gestalt Review,* 14, 1: 71–88.
2. Carlock C. J., Glaus K. O., Shaw S. A. (1992). "The Alcoholic: A Gestalt View", in Nevis E. C. (ed.), *Gestalt Therapy: Perspectives and Applications*, Gardner Press, New York.
3. Francesetti G., Gecele M., Roubal J. (ed.) (2013). *Gestalt Therapy in Clinical Practice: From Psychopathology to the Aesthetics of Contact.* Istituto di Gestalt HCC Italy, Siracusa.
4. Francesetti G. (ed.) (2015). *Absence Is the Bridge Between Us: Gestalt Therapy Perspective on Depressive Experiences.* Istituto di Gestalt HCC Italy, Siracusa.
5. Ginger S., Ginger A. (1987). *La Gestalt, une thérapie du contact.* Hommes et Groupes, Paris.
6. Ginger S. (1995). *La Gestalt, l'art du contact.* Marabout, Paris.
7. Ginger S., Ginger A. (2008). *Guide pratique du psychothérapeute humaniste.* Dunod, Paris.
8. Greenberg E. (2016). *Borderline, Narcissistic, and Schizoid Adaptations: The Pursuit of Love, Admiration, and Safety.* Create Space Independent Publishing Platform, North Charleston.
9. Harris S. (1992). "Gestalt Work With Psychotics", in Nevis E. C. (ed.), *Gestalt Therapy: Perspectives and Applications*, Gardner Press, New York.
10. Joyce P. & Sills C. (2001). *Skills in Gestalt Counselling & Psychotherapy.* SAGE Publications Ltd.

11. Melnick J. & Nevis S. M. (1992). "Diagnosis: The Struggle for a Meaningful Paradigm", in Nevis E. C. (ed.), *Gestalt Therapy: Perspectives and Applications,* Gardner Press, New York.

12. Melnick J. & Nevis S. M. (1997). "Gestalt Diagnosis and DSM IV" *British Gestalt Journal*, 6, 4.

13. Perls F. (1947). *Ego, Hunger and Aggression: A Revision of Freud's Theory and Method.* The Gestalt Journal Press, Inc., Gouldsboro.

14. Perls F., Hefferline R., Goodman P. (1951). *Gestalt Therapy: Excitement and Growth in the Human Personality.* The Gestalt Journal Press, Inc., Gouldsboro.

15. Pintus G. (2017). "Addiction as Persistent Traumatic Experience: Neurobiological Processes and Good Contact" *Gestalt Review*, 21, 3: 221–232.

16. Roubal J. (2007). "Depression. A Gestalt Theoretical Perspective" *British Gestalt Journal*, 16, 1: 35–43.

17. Salathe N. (1988). *Precis de Gestalt-therapie.* Amers. Paris.

18. Schulthess P. (2006). "Addictions, therapie et conseil psycho-social" Addiction. *Revue Gestalt*, 31.

19. Spagnuolo Lobb M. (2002). "A Gestalt Therapy Model for Addressing Psychosis" *British Gestalt Journal*, 11, 1: 5–15.

20. Spagnuolo Lobb M. (2018). "Aesthetic Relational Knowledge of the Field: A Revised Concept of Awareness in Gestalt Therapy and Contemporary Psychiatry" *Gestalt Review*, 22, 1: 50–68.

21. Taylor M. (2014). *Trauma Therapy And Clinical Practice: Neuroscience, Gestalt And The Body.* Open University Press, Milton Keynes, United Kingdom.

22. Yontef, G. (1988). "Assimilating diagnostic and psychoanalytic perspectives into Gestalt therapy". *The Gestalt Journal*, 11, 1, 5-32.

23. Yontef, G. (1993). *Awareness, dialogue & process: Essays on Gestalt therapy.* Gestalt Journal Press. Gouldsboro, ME

24. Yontef G. M. (2001). "Psychotherapy of Schizoid Process." *Transactional Analysis Journal*, 31, 1: 7–23.

Gestalt therapy is a psychotherapeutic approach that particularly values human freedom. Gestalt philosophy offers a path to this freedom through awareness, authenticity and wholeness.

For us Ukrainians, these principles have taken on special significance. This book is being published during dramatic times, when Ukraine is waging war for its sovereignty and existential right to exist as a free nation. The full-scale Russian invasion that began on February 24, 2022, continues to this day, bringing destruction and suffering. The Ukrainian people are resisting occupiers, demonstrating resilience and courage. This ordeal touches every Ukrainian, every Ukrainian family. Ukrainian resilience is strengthened by our people's unity and the support of other countries and specific individuals who support us — our true friends.

I believe that publishing this book in English is very important for the Ukrainian Gestalt community. For the first time, Ukrainian work in Gestalt therapy is being published internationally under the auspices of The Gestalt Journal — a publishing house that has existed since 1977 and has published countless important works in our field. This is not just incredibly important professional recognition for me—it is also a genuine bridge between the Ukrainian and global Gestalt communities, an opportunity to share our work experience while maintaining fidelity to the theory and methodology developed by the founders of our method.

This English-language publication allows Ukrainian Gestalt therapists to enter into international dialogue and show that Ukrainian psychotherapy continues to develop even under wartime conditions.

I am grateful to Molly Rawle and The Gestalt Journal Press for the opportunity to publish this work. The Gestalt Journal Press has remained the leading publisher in the world of Gestalt therapy for decades. I developed as a professional on the books of this publishing house—from the classic works of Fritz and Laura Perls to contemporary works by Gary Yontef and Peter Philippson. It is a great honor for me to become part of this tradition.

I am donating all author royalties from this book to support the Armed Forces of Ukraine and to fund Ukrainian translations of works by international authors in Gestalt therapy. This is my way of thanking those who defend our freedom and making global psychotherapeutic literature more accessible to Ukrainian colleagues.

May this book become not only a source of knowledge, but a symbol that the human spirit, the striving for growth and healing, cannot be broken.

—*Yevgeny Ryaboy*
July 19, 2025

www.ingramcontent.com/pod-product-compliance
Lightning Source LLC
Chambersburg PA
CBHW052025030426
42335CB00026B/3279